The Power of Influence

Life-Changing Lessons from the Coach

Fisher DeBerry

with Mike Burrows

FISHER DeBERRY
FOUNDATION

The Power of Influence
Copyright © 2009 by Fisher DeBerry
Published by the Fisher DeBerry Foundation

Interior photography courtesy of Athletic Department, U.S. Air Force Academy
Design and production by Jeff Lane/Brandango.us

ISBN 978-0-692-00449-4

Printed in the United States of America

6 5 4 3 2 1

I dedicate this book to all the coaches who influenced my life. My philosophies in coaching, my attitudes and my daily walk are the direct result of the seeds you planted.

I also dedicate this book to my family, whom I love dearly and am greatly inspired by every day.

–Fisher DeBerry

To Tim Mimick, a dear friend who died of complications from cancer at age 55 on May 10, 2009, at Genoa (Neb.) Community Hospital. Tim was an award-winning sports writer at the Colorado Springs Gazette, where he worked from 1979–2003. He was the best of the best, on and off the field, and displayed extraordinary courage during the last year of his life. No one has ever admired Air Force coaches and players more than Tim. We love you and we miss you, Tim.

–Mike Burrows

CONTENTS

Acknowledgments

I salute all single parents who display daily courage and commitment to their children to ensure they always have the right opportunities in their lives. You are my heroes.

And thanks as well to Mike Burrows, a man I have admired and respected many years for his great love and passion for writing about sports.

—*Fisher DeBerry*

In the spirit of the great success Air Force Academy football has enjoyed over the years, terrific team effort helped make this book a winner.

This book would not have been possible without the eager, inspiring participation of the many Air Force people who contributed chapters, all of whom played for, coached alongside or worked with Fisher DeBerry. A special salute goes to them, to Wake Forest coach Jim Grobe and to former Baylor coach Grant Teaff, now the executive director of the American Football Coaches Association, for their contributions.

Heartfelt thanks also goes to associate athletic director Troy Garnhart and the Air Force athletic department for providing many of the photographs you see in this book and for helping to make the book available to worldwide fans of the Falcons.

Your wonderful assistance will never be forgotten.

—*Mike Burrows*

JIM GROBE

Wake Forest head football coach
Air Force linebackers coach (1984-94)
Hometown: Huntington, W.Va.
Resides now: Winston-Salem, N.C.

IT WAS OBVIOUS TO EVERYONE THAT JIM WAS DESTINED FOR GREATNESS WHEN HE WAS AN AIR FORCE ASSISTANT COACH. HE LEFT THE ACADEMY TO BE THE HEAD COACH AT OHIO UNIVERSITY AND DID VERY WELL THERE, SO IT'S NO SURPRISE HE HAS HAD SUCH SUCCESS AS WAKE FOREST'S HEAD COACH. HE HAD THE ADMIRATION AND RESPECT OF ALL HIS PLAYERS AT AIR FORCE, AND I'M SURE IT'S THE SAME WITH HIS PLAYERS AT WAKE FOREST. HE NOT ONLY COACHES THEM TO BECOME GOOD PLAYERS; HE COACHES THEM TO BECOME GOOD PEOPLE. HE DISPLAYS IMPECCABLE INTEGRITY, EVIDENCED BY HIS CHAIRMANSHIP OF THE ETHICS COMMITTEE OF THE AMERICAN FOOTBALL COACHES ASSOCIATION.

Most players remember the life-changing lessons they learned while playing for Fisher DeBerry more than the X's and O's, victories or bowl games. What a tribute that is to Coach DeBerry: caring for each other, commitment to team over self and a true feeling of family far outweighed the value of football fundamentals.

The power of positive influence should not be underestimated when studying the success of the Air Force Academy football teams under the guidance of Coach DeBerry. His leadership style stressed the importance of doing everything the right way both on and off the field. Competition and the will to be the best were not just football concepts; players knew they were expected to be great citizens as well as outstanding players.

We were somewhat spoiled as Air Force coaches because of the built-in toughness and discipline so inherent at the academy. The rigors of day-to-day responsibilities are so challenging, cadets considered football practice an enjoyable diversion. While demanding physical and mental excellence is important, it certainly doesn't guarantee moral integrity, Coach DeBerry's specialty.

The faith of Coach DeBerry enabled him to keep the game of football in proper perspective. He believed that developing the whole person would ultimately lead to winning on the field, a concept that filtered down to everyone in the Falcons' football family. Our players understood they were valued to the highest degree regardless of to their performance on the field.

Players developed a remarkable closeness with one another. When the guy at the top displays an unconditional love for his players, it becomes contagious. Facing the challenges of the academy helped to cement the bonds between players. The pursuit of winning at the major college level required that we trust one another.

My 11 years at the Air Force Academy influenced my coaching career tremendously. I watched in awe as Coach DeBerry pushed our players to the breaking point while patting them on the back the entire way. There's a right way to do it, and at Wake Forest, we try to follow the academy blueprint as much as possible.

Coach DeBerry hired me for a position on his staff without an interview. I'm pretty sure that when he called around for recommendations, he spent less time asking about my coaching knowledge and more about how I treated my players. That's how I hire our coaches at Wake Forest. Today, more than ever, kids need coaches who will teach them more than football; they are in need of positive role models.

This book, in the words of some of the players, coaches and staff members who helped to make Air Force a major force in college football, isn't just about the great game we all love. You will read about a great coach, Fisher DeBerry, and the enormous impact he made on his players and fellow coaches. This book is about people, blessed to be associated with Coach DeBerry, who are making the lives of others better by implementing what they learned while at the academy. That's the power of positive influence.

My years at the academy went by in a heartbeat. Leaving Air Force was a career decision nearly impossible to make. Our coaches were as close as the players. I miss those days immensely and cheer for the Falcons in every game they play. The positive influence of Coach DeBerry filters down to everyone associated with Air Force Academy football.

Thank God for Fisher DeBerry. Now there's a football coach!

MIKE BURROWS

Sports writer
University of Nebraska at Kearney
Graduated in 1979
Hometown: Columbus, Neb.
Resides now: Centennial, Colo.

When I covered Air Force Academy football for the Colorado Springs newspaper, The Gazette, during the Fisher DeBerry era, I had it made. My peers were envious. Not only did I cover exciting Air Force teams; I was paid to go on daily excursions to one of the largest, most beautiful college campuses in America. I was surrounded by the best people you could ever hope to meet and know: Air Force players, coaches, administrators and other staff members. I saw firsthand the important role football plays in the extraordinarily difficult four-year journey that turns Air Force cadets into Air Force officers. The man who directed the program had a 23-year record of 169-109-1 and was the winningest coach in the history of military academy football when he retired after the Falcons completed the 2006 season.

Fisher DeBerry used to thank me for coming to practice, for writing about his players, for remembering the noble and patriotic mission of the Air Force

Academy. Now I get to thank him for being the best coach and person I've ever known, and for giving me the sky-high honor of helping produce "The Power of Influence."

This book was never intended to be about Fisher DeBerry, at Fisher's request. When I contacted many of his former players and assistant coaches to participate in this project, I asked them to limit their praise of Coach DeBerry and talk more about other great role models in their lives while reliving memories of their years at the academy. To a man, they all said they would no more limit their praise of Coach DeBerry than they would limit their efforts for the Falcons. So you'll read more about Coach DeBerry than he would prefer.

This book is full of terrific testimonials about the power of influence, spiced with memories of Air Force's strong football heritage; it's also a salute to a great man who has positively impacted the life of every person who's ever known him.

INTRODUCTION

FISHER DeBERRY

"We never know the seeds we sow or the influence we have." Those words are the driving force of this book, produced and published to remind us of the great responsibility we all have to be positive role models.

I recently received telephone calls from two former Air Force Academy football players. The first call was from Spanky Gilliam, who broke the news that his former high school coach had died unexpectedly. "Coach DeBerry," he said, "I'm on my way from New Jersey to Arkansas to attend Coach Steelman's funeral. He had such a profound impact on my life. I would not be who I am today if not for the power of his positive influence."

The other call came from Rodney Lewis. Rodney let me know that the unit under his command had just been voted the best of its kind in the entire Air Force. Rodney was calling to thank everyone who had given him the opportunity to attend and graduate from the Air Force Academy. He wanted me to know that the leadership qualities he acquired as an Academy cadet and player in our football program helped him lead his unit to this great accomplishment.

These are two examples of the hundreds of people who have called and written to me. In their phone calls, both men were quick to acknowledge that it's the influence of the people around them and the seeds that were sown in their young lives that resulted in who they are today.

We all become who we are privileged to know. Many of our leadership techniques and character traits are learned from others. As a coach, I constantly reminded our staff of the awesome responsibility we had as coaches to be a positive influence on the lives of our players. Sometimes a coach is the only father figure in a young man's life, and a team is the only family identification a young man can claim.

I was the product of a single-parent family in rural Cheraw, S.C. Primarily because of the love, support and encouragement I received from my coaches, I made coaching my life's work and enjoyed 44 years in the coaching profession, including 23 years as the head coach of the Air Force Academy football team. My coaches were my heroes, and they filled the role of a father in my life. Each exemplified the leader and the role model I wanted to become.

As you read this book, created from the testimonials of many Air Force players, coaches and staff members, challenge yourself to be a positive role model, to be a strong influence on the lives of people around you. There is no greater reward, no better way to live. You don't have to be a football coach or know a tackle from a turnover to be a positive role model. Anybody can be one, provided you first embrace the responsibility. Peer pressure and influence are the most powerful forces in the world today. With a dose of love, those forces can positively change lives.

I hope you love this book and enjoy reliving some great memories of Air Force football with many of the terrific players, coaches and staff members who made it happen. Hopefully, everyone who reads this book will be inspired by the terrific testimonials and become more aware of — and responsible for — the influence you make on the precious lives of those around you.

Proceeds from this book go directly to the Fisher DeBerry Foundation, a tax-exempt, nonprofit organization dedicated to the life-changing support and education of single parents and their children. Our foundation provides support for parenting development, mentoring programs, after-school activities and academic scholarships. You can find out more at www.FisherDeBerryFoundation.org.

CHAPTER ONE

FISHER DEBERRY

Head coach (1984–2006)
Offensive coordinator (1981–83)
Quarterbacks coach (1980)
Hometown: Cheraw, S.C.
Resides now: Isle of Palms, S.C.

SINCE RETIRING FROM ACTIVE COACHING AT THE END OF THE 2006 SEASON, I HAVE HAD A LOT OF TIME TO REFLECT ON MY 44 YEARS IN THE PROFESSION. I CONCLUDED THAT YOU QUICKLY FORGET THE WINS AND THE LOSSES. WHAT LASTS FOREVER ARE THE RELATIONSHIPS WITH THE PLAYERS AND COACHES I HAD THE PLEASURE OF WORKING WITH AND KNOWING AS A FAMILY. THEIR LIVES HAVE GREATLY INFLUENCED MY LIFE, AND I WILL BE ETERNALLY THANKFUL FOR THE OPPORTUNITIES AND TIMES WE HAD TOGETHER. WE NEVER REALIZE OR KNOW THE POWERFUL INFLUENCE THAT OTHERS HAVE ON US OR THAT WE MIGHT HAVE HAD ON THEM. WE OFTEN DON'T REALIZE THE FRUITS OF THE SEEDS WE SOW UNTIL LATER IN LIFE.

Last spring, I was in the city where I coached high school football and baseball to plan a golf tournament that would raise funds for our foundation, which benefits children in single-parent families. I had coached several former players who were living in this community, and they agreed to help. Walking into the first meeting, I saw a player I had not seen in almost 40 years. As we embraced, the first thing Charlie asked was, "Coach, how many garden seeds have you said today?" I couldn't believe he was asking this after all these years. Garden seed was a term I used, instead of profanity, to get my point across to the players.

In my interaction with young people, I sense there are three things they really want from adults. First, they want a positive role model they can look up to and depend on. Next, they want family stability. And third, they want discipline. This is why I believe athletics play such an important role in a young person's life. Athletics might be the last stronghold of discipline.

Before our marriage, my wife, Lu Ann, lived with a wonderful lady named Mrs. Mayfield while she was teaching high school business. Mrs. Mayfield was such a charming, witty and inspiring lady. We spent many hours on her porch talking. When Lu Ann and I would leave to go to a movie or to see friends, Mrs. Mayfield would always say, "Remember who you are." Her words made a lasting impression on me, and I later shared those words with my own children. It's a reminder that as responsible and caring adults, we have an enormous responsibility for our role, for our influence, in the lives of the people around us.

In the master playbook, the Holy Bible, we know from reading Matthew 5:16 to "let your light shine before men, that they may see your good deeds and praise your Father in heaven." To me, "light" means our everyday walk, the role model we are to others by the way we live our own lives.

I would like to share a poem with you that speaks to me in a mighty way about the responsibility we have to others as fathers, mothers, coaches and friends. The title of the poem is "To Any Athlete," but the title could just as easily be "To Any Coach, Parent or Businessperson."

To Any Athlete
Author Unknown

There are little eyes upon you and they're watching night and day,
and there are little ears that take in every word you say.

There are little hands all eager to do anything you do
and a little boy who's dreaming of the day he'll be like you.

You're the little fellow's idol, you're the wisest of the wise;
in his mind about you no suspicions ever arise.

He believes in you devoutly, holds all that you say and do.
He will say and do in your own way when he's a grownup like you.

There's a wide-eyed little fellow who believes you're always right,
and his ears are always open and he watches day and night.

You are setting an example every day in all you do,
for the little boy who's waiting to grow up to be just like you.

What an awesome responsibility we have! We often do not discover the
result of the seeds sown — the influence we are making — until years down the
road. Then we might get a message that reminds us, as I did one day out of
the clear blue. It was an e-mail from Tony, a former player of mine. Tony did
not finish the academy. He was a great player, but he developed a disqualifying
medical condition. I helped him finish his education at another great university,
where he played outstanding football. In this e-mail, Tony thanked me for my
support, for everything he learned while at the academy, and for all the great
memories. Tony shared that he was now a Baptist youth minister. I immediately
wrote back and told Tony how proud we were of him and his positive influence
on young people, and that we would be praying for him in his work with the
youth of his church in Tennessee.

In another e-mail, he informed me that Shane, his best friend at the
academy, became a youth minister as well. Shane didn't graduate from the
academy either, and I had helped him get an opportunity at the University of
Tennessee, where he became an all-Southeastern Conference player. He was
selected in the third round of the NFL draft and had an excellent pro career, and
he had been greatly influenced by Tony.

I would see Tony and Shane again at the opening game of our 2006 season,
when Air Force played Tennessee in Knoxville. I asked them to stop by our locker
room after the game and join our postgame ritual.

That night, we lost a 31-30 thriller to the Volunteers before 106,000
fans at Neyland Stadium. In the locker room, disappointment hung over the
players like a dark cloud. Eventually, the last people left in our locker room
were Tony, Shane and me. I told them I was proud of them, and they shared
how much influence the academy and playing football had on their lives and

on helping them become youth ministers.

That locker-room experience challenged me to ask other Air Force players and coaches to share their stories about people of influence in their lives and to collect them in book form to share with others. May this book encourage you to consider the power of your influence in the lives of the people you know.

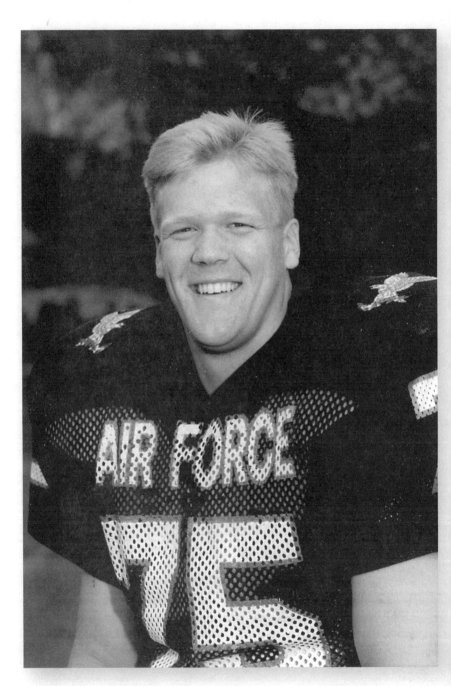

CHAPTER TWO

MAJ. TOM KAFKA

Defensive lineman
Three-year letterman (1987–89)
Graduated in 1990
Hometown: Omaha, Neb.
Resides now: Panama City, Fla.

TOUGH AND STEADY, THAT WAS TOMMY AS AN AIR FORCE PLAYER. TOMMY ALWAYS PLAYED HIS TOUGHEST FOOTBALL IN THE REALLY BIG GAMES. HE WAS A VERY DEPENDABLE PLAYER AND ALWAYS PAID CLOSE ATTENTION TO DETAIL, SO HIS OUTSTANDING CAREER AS AN AIR FORCE PILOT DOESN'T SURPRISE ANYONE. HE WAS ONE OF OUR TEAM CAPTAINS AS A SENIOR IN 1989, WHICH TELLS YOU THE HIGH LEVEL OF RESPECT HE HAD FROM HIS TEAMMATES.

I am the only F-22 Raptor pilot who has had THR surgery. THR is an acronym for total hip replacement, and I had that surgery at the academy hospital when I was only 34. Playing major college football, especially as a lineman, isn't easy to do. The constant pounding associated with playing my position eventually took a toll, requiring me to undergo a surgery commonly associated with senior citizens. Now you know why I believe the Air Force Academy is the best place to learn how to overcome adversity and how to meet challenges head-on.

Active-duty fighter pilots who have had joint-replacement surgery are rare. Not only was I concerned about being able to continue my military career as a proud pilot, but I was also concerned about being able to stay in the military. I had memorized three simple words while attending the Air Force Academy and playing football for Coach DeBerry and the Falcons: Never give up! These helped immensely in my recovery from THR and quickened my return to the cockpit. I'm still a proud pilot today, flying the world's No. 1 fighter jet, a $135 million marvel of a machine.

Never give up! Those words have never left me. They helped me get through basic cadet training at the academy, a remarkably grueling period that precedes each cadet's freshman year, and they guided me through to graduation. They also guided me through intense pilot training and helped me pass the exhaustive test of learning to fly the famed F-15 Eagle, which I flew before advancing to the stealth F-22.

Coach DeBerry and my father are at the top of my list when it comes to people who have had the biggest influence on my life. That's quite a statement, considering the great leadership you find throughout the U.S. Air Force. Coach DeBerry and my father possess an intensely optimistic passion for life and for people. They both care more about others than they do about themselves. They both treat everyone the same. It doesn't matter if they're talking to a four-star general, to an Air Force airman or to a custodian. They believe all people are of equal importance and deserve to be treated with respect. I try to follow those values in my Air Force career, especially as an officer who represents the power of influence. Believe me, it is something I don't take lightly.

Playing football at Air Force taught me many valuable life lessons. Air Force Falcons win and lose with equal dignity. Air Force Falcons don't give up, no matter how daunting the challenge. Air Force Falcons get the most out of their ability. Air Force Falcons are coachable and go the extra mile to improve. Air Force Falcons never take a play off. Air Force Falcons treat practices with the importance of games.

I use these lessons daily as an F-22 instructor pilot at Tyndall Air Force Base near Panama City, Fla. Teaching pilots how to fly and fight in the F-22 is similar to playing Falcon football. You have to come to work (or practice) every day determined to prove you deserve to be part of the fighter squadron (or team). No one cares what you did on your last flight (or your last play). It only matters what you do on your next flight (or next play). Air Force football players risk injury playing a demanding game to make sure the Falcons are successful. F-22 pilots place their lives on the line to make sure the squadron is successful. All squadrons and teams are only as good as their weakest link. That's the newest pilot in a squadron and the least experienced player on a team. When they achieve success, everyone in the squadron or team benefits.

I often think back to my Air Force football career while preparing for a flight. My fondest memories include what took place after each practice. Coach DeBerry would tell the players to gather around him and "take a knee." Then he would talk to us, sometimes for as long as 30 minutes, not just as a coach but as a father figure. The epitome of Southern grace and charm, Coach DeBerry would tell us, among many important things, to "go call your momma and tell her that you love her, and thank her for making you the man you are today. For without her, you wouldn't be here today." I've never forgotten that.

After my hip-replacement surgery in February 2002, I was back flying the F-15 by July of that same year. I became the fifth or sixth pilot ever to fly fighters after having THR surgery. This surgery took place more than 12 years after I completed my football career at the Air Force Academy, yet Coach DeBerry was one of the first visitors I had in my hospital room after the surgery. Even though no games are being played, February is a busy month for the Air Force football program, with recruiting in full gear and preparations being made for spring practices. Yet Coach DeBerry stayed in my hospital room for several hours, talking with me. Now there's the power of influence in its purest form.

Never give up!

Chapter Three

MARC MUNAFO

Halfback
Three-year letterman (1984–86)
Graduated in 1987
Hometown: Huron, Ohio
Resides now: Florida Keys

MARC WAS A CLASSIC EXAMPLE OF THE SUCCESS THAT COMES WHEN YOU TAKE ADVANTAGE OF YOUR OPPORTUNITY. HE MADE SURE TO BE PREPARED WHEN THE TIME CAME TO CONTRIBUTE TO THE SUCCESS OF THE TEAM. HIS SMILE AND LOVE OF THE GAME ALWAYS INSPIRED ME AND HIS TEAMMATES. IN 1986, HIS SENIOR SEASON, MARC NEEDED ONLY 17 CARRIES TO GAIN 120 YARDS (7.1 YARDS PER RUSH) IN OUR 23-21 VICTORY AT TEXAS-EL PASO. AND AS YOU WILL DISCOVER WHEN YOU READ HIS CHAPTER, MARC IS AN EXTRAORDINARILY TALENTED WRITER.

Some men cast a giant shadow over your whole life. You hear their voice, picture their gaze and think about how they would handle a given situation long after their physical presence has retired. Some leaders can even affect you in a mere moment in time. That moment can then expand and become a way of life.

For men, such impact and lasting influence can only be derived from pain, sweat, toil and, ultimately, fulfillment. I believe the strongest bonds between men are forged through adversity. The memory of one man, one leader, can help guide you through all of life's future battles.

I was lucky. I played for Fisher DeBerry and the United States Air Force Academy. It's funny; I can't remember a single page from our playbook. I don't recall how Coach DeBerry taught me to "arc block" or pick up a blitzing linebacker, catch with my hands or cover the ball. No, even though I have so many wonderful memories of Coach DeBerry and playing for the Falcons, what I remember most is one specific moment in time.

One game in 1985 during my junior season, the player ahead of me became injured and had to leave the game. Up to that point, I had played only on special teams or when we were ahead by 40 points. This was a big game against BYU, and it was going down to the wire. As I realized my proving time arrived, I felt as if someone had suddenly tied a perfect sheepshank in my large intestine. Several voices yelled my name as I quickly deduced that while in uniform I couldn't blend into the crowd well enough to escape. I approached the sideline wearing my false bravado like a coat of armor.

Coach DeBerry reached up and gently took hold of my face mask. "This is *your* time," he said. "Are you ready, Marc?"

It was not a rhetorical question. Coach DeBerry's grip on my face mask was neutral, as if he could evenly toss me back to the sideline or out to the playing field, depending on my answer. His expression was one that I will never forget. His eyes were intense yet curious, and I could detect a little twinkle, like a glint of humor. He had half a smile on his face, and he looked rapt, as though he could stand there all day waiting for my answer. He knew me. He knew all his players. He didn't need to explain the importance of the situation. He didn't need to flatter me or threaten me. No pep talk was necessary. He knew those tactics wouldn't work.

At that moment it was just him and me. The crowd, the other players and the noise all vanished. The way Coach DeBerry posed that question and the expression on his face took me by surprise, and I actually paused before I answered in the affirmative. He nudged my face mask toward the huddle and gave me a little wink. My colon uncoiled, and the nervousness drained away as I jogged out toward my teammates. I felt 10 feet tall.

I played some of the best football of my life that day.

Coach somehow knew that all I needed at that exact moment was nothing more than his faith. He wasn't asking me if I was ready to play football that day. He was asking me if I was ready to become a man in his world. As comparatively unimportant as that game may have been to the rest of the world, Coach DeBerry knew it was the defining moment in my young life because it would put my fledgling character to the test. I can't prove it, but I believe Coach was more concerned about how that testing moment would prepare me for life's future trials. That's the real testament to Coach DeBerry: Football was just a means to developing character and molding leaders.

Today, it is my turn to lead, and I often wonder whether all leaders are merely emulating someone from their past as I try to emulate Coach DeBerry. I will never have his boundless, perpetual energy or his repertoire of homespun Carolina wisdom. (No one could mangle a metaphor quite like Fisher.) But I can aspire to uphold his impeccable integrity, unparalleled work ethic and faith in the goodness of God and man. And one day, I pray that a moment from my life will inspire a leader from the next generation as well. Influence is passed down through the generations like a fine coin collection. If properly handled and nurtured, it becomes more valuable with each successive owner.

CHAPTER FOUR

BRYCE FISHER

———

Defensive lineman
Two-year letterman (1997–98)
Graduated in 1999
Hometown: Renton, Wash.
Resides now: Kirkland, Wash.

———

A LATE BLOOMER, BRYCE HAD A LONG CAREER IN THE NFL AFTER DEVELOPING INTO ONE OF THE NATION'S BEST DEFENSIVE LINEMEN. IT WAS GREAT TO SEE ALL HIS HARD WORK PAY OFF. HE WAS A ROCK ON AIR FORCE'S 12-1 TEAM IN 1998, WHICH WON THE WESTERN ATHLETIC CONFERENCE CHAMPIONSHIP HIS SENIOR SEASON. BRYCE WAS THE AIR FORCE PLAYER WHO SURPRISED ME THE MOST. WHEN HE ARRIVED AT THE ACADEMY, HE WAS ROLY-POLY AND DIDN'T MEET THE VISUAL STANDARDS OF A DIVISION I-A PLAYER. I EVEN BET OUR COACHES THAT HE WOULDN'T STAY. BUT ONCE HE DECIDED HE WANTED TO BE A DIVISION I-A PLAYER, HE PUT IN THE TIME AND EFFORT TO DEVELOP HIS BODY AND SKILLS. BRYCE ENDED UP BEING A POPULAR PLAYER AND LEADER. HE IS PROOF THAT YOU CAN ACHIEVE ANYTHING IF YOU WANT IT BADLY ENOUGH.

———

"Remember who you are and who you represent." After every game, win or lose, Coach DeBerry would say those eight words to us. And those eight words were enough. We won a lot of games when I played for the Falcons, going 10-3 my junior year in 1997 and 12-1 my senior year in 1998 as Western Athletic Conference champions. But the outcomes of our games were almost irrelevant to what Coach DeBerry built at the Air Force Academy. From my recruiting trip through my graduation, he taught his players it was the brotherhood that mattered most.

"If you can't do it for yourself, do it for your brother," Coach DeBerry said. And we did just that. On the field, in the classroom and in the community, our bond was unbreakable and remains so today. That is his lasting legacy, his power of influence.

Beyond all the victories and the Commander-in-Chief's trophies, Coach DeBerry and his staff truly helped mold men. We were all a little small and a little slow, but because we had such a belief in each other, we could stand toe to toe with Goliath. One of the assistants, Coach Richard Bell, used to say that hustle and preparation were talents just as valuable as speed and strength. It wasn't until I was in the NFL for a couple of years that I fully understood what he was saying. I probably was a little short in natural athletic ability compared with most defensive ends in the NFL. But what I had that many others didn't was the unshakable belief that I could out-prepare and out hustle anyone on my way to success. That cornerstone of Air Force football helped me play seven seasons in the NFL, starting with the Buffalo Bills in 2001 and including moves to the St. Louis Rams, Seattle Seahawks and Tennessee Titans, my most recent team.

My sophomore year at Air Force, we were preparing to play the Fighting Irish at Notre Dame Stadium. Lou Holtz, Ron Powlus, Touchdown Jesus and all that nonsense. They had killed us 44-14 the year before at Falcon Stadium, and we were supposed to be another easy win for the Irish in 1996. Our defensive coaching staff installed a totally new defense we had never seen. Not a new wrinkle or adjustment, but a completely new defensive front and coverage. We quickly learned the new defense on Monday the week of the Notre Dame game and then practiced it on Tuesday, Wednesday and Thursday. Saturday arrived, and we beat the Irish 20-17 in overtime on national television. Even though I didn't play in that game, it remains one of my favorite memories from my Air Force career. I believe because that Air Force team was able to beat Notre Dame but couldn't beat Army or Navy in 1996, we were spurred to recommit ourselves to excellence, fueling our remarkable 22-4 run in the 1997 and 1998 seasons.

Saturday workouts became routine, practices were more competitive and our collective will was forged.

Almost a decade has passed since my time at the Air Force Academy, but my memories of that wonderful place remain as clear as if it were yesterday. Our brotherhood has been stretched across the globe and two wars, but we are never more than a phone call or an e-mail message away from one another.

Coach DeBerry, for all the hills you made us run, for the extra instruction on the plane coming home from road games, and even for the time you made us wear our service dress for eight hours while flying back from Hawaii, thank you. I am a better person for being an Air Force Falcon and playing for you.

CHAPTER FIVE

RICHARD BELL

———

Inside linebackers coach (1995–2006)
Defensive coordinator (1999–2006)
Hometown: Little Rock, Ark.
Resides now: Smyrna, Ga.

———

COACHES AND PEOPLE DON'T COME ANY BETTER THAN RICHARD, WHO WAS A TERRIFIC ADDITION TO THE AIR FORCE COACHING STAFF. RICHARD WAS A GREAT MOLDER OF MEN AND ONE OF THE BEST COACHES EVER IN DIVISION I-A FOOTBALL ON THE DEFENSIVE SIDE OF THE BALL. HE WAS A WONDERFUL EXAMPLE AND ROLE MODEL FOR ALL THE TEAMS HE COACHED. RICHARD COACHED BECAUSE HIS FIRST LOVE WAS HIS PLAYERS. HE PERSONIFIES WHAT THE CORE OF THIS BOOK IS ALL ABOUT. HE WAS A TIRELESS WORKER WHO WAS MORE THAN JUST AN ALWAYS-PREPARED COACH. A GREAT FRIEND AND CHRISTIAN BROTHER, THAT'S RICHARD.

———

When I became head football coach at South Carolina in January 1982, the first call I made was to Fisher DeBerry. I wanted this man, who was assistant coach at the Air Force Academy, to join my staff. Fisher listened to my offer but ultimately declined, choosing to remain at the academy. Although I was disappointed, there was no question Fisher made the right decision, because a year later, he was promoted to head coach at the Air Force Academy, beginning the Falcons' very successful Fisher DeBerry era.

Through the years that followed, we crossed paths from time to time. I was not surprised at his success, yet when I stopped and thought about what he was accomplishing, it truly was an amazing achievement. Year in and year out, Fisher and his staff caused a group of young men to excel and achieve above their talent level. The consistency with which his Air Force teams won and whom they won against — the tough Western Athletic Conference, and Texas, Virginia Tech, Mississippi State, Notre Dame and Ohio State — continued to raise my curiosity as to what made this man and his AFA teams so special. Whenever we did talk in person or by phone, I was always greatly impressed with his humility, his desire to give his staff credit and his sincere, bold stand to give the Lord Jesus praise for any success he had achieved. Our brief encounters made me look forward to longer periods of time together so I could truly know the man and the philosophy he lived and competed by.

Following the 1994 football season at Navy, where I was the defensive coordinator, I called Fisher to recommend one of our coaches for a position on his staff at Air Force. After discussing his qualifications, I was about to end the conversation when Fisher asked about *my* interest in a position on his staff. I didn't realize he had a position open on his defensive staff, but there was no question the Lord had opened the door for this opportunity. So in January 1995, my wife, Marilyn, and I began a special 12-year adventure with Fisher and his wife, Lu Ann, and the quality men and their families who made up the Air Force family.

1995 was a learning year for me as I came to know the players and staff I had long admired from a distance. I saw the work ethic, the effort and the intangibles I associated with winning, but I didn't really begin to understand what made Air Force football special until our season-opening game against Brigham Young. The Falcons were coming off an 8-4 season, and in our morning staff meeting preceding the 1995 opener, Coach DeBerry asked each assistant coach to share what he honestly thought about our chances in the game that Saturday. As each coach responded, I could tell they were excited and thought we had a chance to be a good football team. When my turn came, I couldn't help expressing my concern because I just didn't see what the rest of the staff visualized. To be honest, I just didn't think we were that good. But that

Saturday, I saw I had underestimated our team, as we soundly beat BYU 38-12 at Falcon Stadium.

For the first time in my coaching career, I re-evaluated the definition of "true talent." Yes, talent always will be physical ability, but it is so much more than that. I failed to realize that hustle is a talent, effort is a talent, toughness is a talent, perseverance is a talent and heart is a talent. These intangible talents always take physical talents to a level that physical ability alone can never achieve.

I would continue to learn and grow throughout the season and the years ahead from Air Force players who hungered to make the impossible possible and the unbelievable reality. We went 8-5 in 1995, completing the season in the Copper Bowl against Texas Tech.

I hesitate to begin to name individual players because, honestly, hundreds come to my mind as I think about what unique contributions were made by so many. To each and every one, I salute and offer my appreciation for the lessons I learned from you and your willingness to raise your ability to the level I demanded without complaint.

Frustration would probably be the best word to describe our 1996 season. We all knew we could have achieved so much more than a 6-5 record because we showed our ability to win with intensity and perseverance against Notre Dame (20-17) and Fresno State (44-38), both on the road. We defeated a Fighting Irish team that had overwhelmed a very good Washington Huskies team by rushing for more than 350 yards the week before in a 54-20 rout. The plan Cal McCombs put together was a defensive masterpiece. We held the bigger, stronger Irish to 67 yards rushing at Notre Dame Stadium and beat them in overtime with a field goal.

The week following our 23-7 loss to Army at West Point, we were back on the road to play a very good Fresno State team. To say the first half was a nightmare would be a gross understatement. To the shock of the staff, we left the field at halftime on the short end of a 31-3 score. The shock of the first half only set the stage for one of the greatest comebacks in Air Force history. Late in the game, we tied the Bulldogs 38-38 to take the game into overtime. Fresno State had the ball first in overtime, our defense forced a fumble, and we scored on our possession to win a truly unbelievable game. One of our defensive tackles, Joe Suhajda, will be remembered by the staff and players as "Overtime Joe," because in both the Notre Dame game and the Fresno State game, he created the fumbles in overtime that enabled us to win.

From a year that didn't fulfill our expectations, I still came away encouraged by the "never say die" spirit of our players. These guys loved to play the game, and regardless of how hopeless the situation looked, they played every down with the belief they would find a way to win.

In 1997 we played Colorado State at Fort Collins in the fourth game of the season. The Rams had beaten us 42-41 in a heartbreaker the year before. We were 3-0 as we went into the rematch seeking to find our personality as a young team. That night we discovered who we were in a big way. The offense controlled the ball with no mistakes, and our defense shut down the highly touted Colorado State offense. We won 24-0. You talk about defensive dominance! We had a pass rush called "Thunder," which we called about every long-yardage situation, and that night our great linebacker Chris Gizzi was just impossible for CSU to block. He ran over them, through them and around them to totally frustrate the Rams' offense. The iron will of the Falcons was tested that night, and victory was achieved because a bunch of guys had prepared their wills to withstand any pain to walk off that field as winners.

Many games come to mind that define the character of the remarkable Air Force football program. The victories in 1998 over CSU (Blane Morgan refused to let us lose), Wyoming (none of us will ever forget Spanky Gilliam's third-down run), Rice (Mike Tyler returning an interception for the win on a knee that had a torn ACL), and BYU (Jemal Singleton's block on Rob Morris in the WAC championship game). In 2003 we broke a 22-year precedent with our first victory over BYU in Provo (24-10). In 2006 the Falcons atoned for our 27-24 loss to Army the year before with a 43-7 victory over the Black Knights in an ESPN-televised game at West Point. These great memories stir within me as I replay the 12 wonderful years of coaching at the Air Force Academy with Fisher DeBerry.

Coaching was my chosen vocation when I graduated from the University of Arkansas after playing for the Razorbacks because I loved the competitive aspects of football and hoped to become a positive influence on young men as so many coaches had been on me. To me, the game of football parallels life more than any other endeavor I know. The demand to turn obstacles into opportunities and defeats into victories is a requirement for success on the football field and in life. I was fortunate to have so many great men as my mentors. Each coach I had from junior high school through college was a positive influence on me as a man and a coach.

The impact of the coaches and players I had the privilege to work with at Air Force enabled me to continue growing into the man and coach I desired to become. I firmly believe the success of Air Force football under Fisher can be attributed to the following:

- Placing within the minds and souls of the players that if they believed it, they could achieve it.
- The realization that we may not have had the best athletes, but we had the best team. You don't need to have the best players; you have to have the *right* players.
- The contagious enthusiasm of Fisher. The entire team became highly energized, and this enthusiasm increased each player's accomplishments.
- A toughness that defined pain as a friend. Pain was always temporary; quitting was never an option. Success was the mental and physical toughness that demanded you play through pain. Finish! With honor!
- The belief that we were all part of something bigger than each of us. Individually we were important; together we were unbeatable.

Any success I achieved in coaching is directly related to the new life I found when I accepted Jesus as my Lord and Savior when I was 26 years old and on the staff at Georgia Tech. When I discovered that Christianity was not a religion but a relationship with a living Lord Jesus, my life took on new meaning. My roles as husband, father, coach and friend became defined by the truth of God's living Word. Players became human beings with worth and value; I began to see the face behind the helmet and the heart behind the jersey. The words I had mouthed with little sincerity became the creed I coached by: "A player doesn't care how much you know until he knows how much you care." Instead of tearing down my players, I sought to build them up. My hunger to win and to honor the Lord in my vocation increased unbelievably. He gave me a new spirit to never give up, an unflinching will, a heart that saw every setback as an opportunity, and a new passion that demanded I stretch myself to the limit daily in order to grow into the man He desired.

I grew in my faith at the Air Force Academy because of Fisher's example and his desire to see that the program truly honored the Lord. The voluntary share time we had every Wednesday morning during the season was a source of strength to me. To step back from the pressures of preparing for a game for 30 or 45 minutes to talk, to pray, to study with other coaches and friends was uplifting and encouraging. To hear men genuinely open their hearts to express events of praise and situations of concern drew me closer to these men and enabled us to keep our priorities in the proper order. He didn't demand that our players buy into his

Christian faith, but he wasn't going to separate his walk with the Lord from being the head football coach.

A key to any head coach's success is to be able to put together a loyal, knowledgeable, focused and compatible staff. Fisher had a great talent for achieving the proper balance in the men that comprised his staff throughout his career. For all of you who were there with me, my thanks for your friendship, support and encouragement through 12 special years.

We worked hard to achieve the success we were blessed with, and we sure had fun along the way. I won a bunch of dollars off you guys. Marilyn appreciated the extra bucks that enabled us to enjoy a few meals out, due to your willingness to give the old man some much-needed points above the point spread. Always remember you are just a phone call away from losing any surplus cash you may be willing to part with.

Coach DeBerry's famous quotes will always live in our hearts and minds, bringing a smile when we think about our Air Force days:

- "If you see a turtle on the fence post, you know he didn't get there by himself."
- "You're gonna eat till it ouches you."
- "Doolie Wampus." (Used by Fisher when talking about anyone whose name he couldn't remember.)
- "Most of the time when you're ahead at the end of the fourth quarter, you're gonna win the dadgum ball game."
- "Ninety-nine times out of 10."
- "They showed up looking like Hooligan's goat."
- "We think he'll be a better offensive lineman than a center."

Thanks, Fisher, for keeping us loose and laughing when times were tough.

Fisher would lead everyone to believe it was his staff and players who made him look good. But we knew it was his vision, his system and his inspiration that enabled Air Force to enjoy tremendous success. In the environment of a service academy with the academic demands, the recruiting limitations and the military commitment, he found a way to win.

To all his coaching peers, Fisher is a legend whose record speaks for itself. In his 23 years as Air Force's head coach, he won more games (169) than any other service-academy football coach (Air Force, Army or Navy) ever won. Stop to consider the outstanding coaches at Army and Navy that he surpassed — Red Blaik, Jim Young, Paul Dietzel, Eddie Erdelatz, Wayne Hardin and George Welsh, to name a few — you can't help but be impressed with the success the Falcons enjoyed under Fisher's stellar leadership.

These are the wonderful traits that I believe were the foundation of this special coach:

- A system Fisher believed in and never wavered from: an innovative option offense
- An attacking defense and a big-play kicking game
- Inexhaustible energy. Fisher could just go and go and go.
- A sincere concern for people, even in the midst of a heated season. Fisher could pull back, and if someone was hurting, he had time to call or stop by.
- Fisher's willingness to stand by his players when others were ready to give up on them. Because he fought hard for them, they fought hard for him.
- An unbelievably positive attitude. When a player wasn't able to play for a year because of an honor-code violation, or when we lost someone because of an injury, Fisher might have been down for five minutes, but then he would look for the rainbow somewhere within the situation. Fisher simply refused to live under a dark cloud.

To all the players I was privileged to coach, remember to live with this one thing in mind: Never — *never* — let anything that doesn't have a heart whip you.

CHAPTER SIX

DEE DOWIS

Quarterback
Four-year letterman (1986–89)
Graduated in 1990
Junior varsity offensive coordinator (1995–98)
Hometown: Royston, Ga.
Resides now: Greenville, S.C.

DEE MIGHT HAVE BEEN THE MOST EXCITING PLAYER IN THE HISTORY
OF AIR FORCE FOOTBALL. HE HAD REMARKABLE QUICKNESS AND
THE POTENTIAL TO BREAK A BIG PLAY EVERY TIME HE CARRIED THE BALL.
HE AVERAGED 6.7 YARDS PER RUSH DURING HIS CAREER AND STILL IS THE
FALCONS' ALL-TIME LEADING RUSHER WITH 3,612 YARDS. HE FINISHED
SIXTH IN HEISMAN TROPHY VOTING HIS SENIOR SEASON, A GREAT TRIBUTE
TO A GREAT PLAYER. HE WASN'T BIG IN STATURE, BUT HE WAS A GIANT
OF A PLAYER WITH THE BALL IN HIS HANDS. HIS HEART AND PASSION
OUTWEIGHED HIS BODY. GOING TO SEE DEE WAS ONE OF MY MOST
MEMORABLE RECRUITING VISITS, EATING HIS MAMA'S PECAN PIE AND
DRINKING SWEET TEA ON THEIR PORCH.

I don't mind telling you that I was the most unlikely major college football player.
My dream of playing major college football was bigger than I was. My senior

season in high school, I weighed only 145 pounds. When my senior season ended, I thought I had played my last competitive football game. I could picture myself at West Point, playing quarterback for Army, but I guess the Black Knights couldn't picture me playing quarterback for them.

The Falcons got to me extremely late in the recruiting process, but I wasn't about to hold that against them. Not after seeing the beautiful Air Force Academy on a recruiting trip and meeting head coach Fisher DeBerry and his terrific assistants. A coach at a rival high school knew Cal McCombs, who was Air Force's defensive-backs coach at the time, and he told Coach McCombs about me. In a great example of sportsmanship, that rival high school coach helped put me in the best place possible, even though I had serious second thoughts about being at Air Force during an extremely difficult first year that all academy freshmen endure.

I really had no idea what I was getting into. I earned good grades in high school, so I expected to do well academically at Air Force. I thought I could handle the pressure militarily as well. I viewed Air Force as my ticket to playing major college football and serving my country. But to say my freshman year at the academy was rough would be an understatement. Every day was a struggle.

Football practice was the best part of my day. I was 1,500 miles away from my small hometown of Royston, Ga., yet Coach DeBerry's distinctly Southern background helped transport a little bit of home to the dry climate of Colorado Springs. But football was just one part of my day at Air Force. "I'm going home, and then I'm transferring to Georgia Tech or Vanderbilt," I told myself. But I just couldn't pull the trigger.

My parents had one huge rule in our house when I was growing up: You never quit. No exceptions. You never quit anything you start. Every time I thought about leaving the academy, I thought about my parents and their rule. It turned out to be a golden rule for me, because to this day I'm grateful to them and God that I never left the Air Force Academy.

The biggest life lesson I learned while playing football for the Falcons is that you don't back down from a challenge. Instead, you embrace it. We rarely had more talent than the teams we played; yet we had remarkable success. We didn't play for scholarships; we just loved to play. Nobody played harder than we did, and trust me, we were never outcoached. We were led by Fisher DeBerry, a great role model.

My senior season at Air Force was 1989, and our record was 6-0 when Notre Dame, the defending national champion, arrived at Falcon Stadium to play us.

Notre Dame had 10 times the talent we had, and we lost 41-27. But we gave Lou Holtz and the Fighting Irish all they wanted. They went back to South Bend knowing the Falcons had given them a four-quarter fight. I was crushed that we lost, but I was so proud of our effort. We never quit.

After nine years of proud active-duty service as an Air Force officer, I transitioned into the business world, where I use everything I learned at the academy on a daily basis. I'm a district manager for Pfizer, the pharmaceutical company, where I oversee a hardworking group of 12 people. They know what I stand for, and everything I stand for comes from my family, from playing football for Coach DeBerry and from being an Air Force cadet. You don't achieve anything good in life without hard work. And you have a responsibility to make a positive impact on other lives, whether it's as a husband, a father, a co-worker, a teammate, a friend, a soldier or a volunteer.

CHAPTER SEVEN

PAT EVANS

———

Fullback
Three-year letterman (1984–86)
Graduated in 1987
Junior-varsity defensive coordinator (1993–94)
Hometown: Vicksburg, Miss.
Resides now: Wildwood, Mo.

———

PAT WAS THE DEFINITION OF A HARD-NOSED FULLBACK AND A TERRIFIC TEAM PLAYER. HE RUSHED FOR 1,015 YARDS AS A SOPHOMORE IN 1984, MY FIRST SEASON AS AIR FORCE'S HEAD COACH, AND THEN HAD TO OVERCOME A SERIOUS KNEE INJURY IN 1985. HE LED THE FALCONS IN RUSHING AGAIN IN 1986, HIS SENIOR SEASON. PAT WAS THE BEST PRACTICE PLAYER I EVER COACHED. THAT WAS THE REASON HE PLAYED SO WELL EACH SATURDAY. PAT PREPARED SO HARD DURING THE WEEK, HIS INTENSITY WAS THE SAME IN PRACTICES AS IT WAS IN GAMES. HE BELIEVED HE WAS GOOD BECAUSE HE WORKED SO HARD TO BE GOOD. HIS PARENTS DIDN'T MISS BUT ONE GAME HIS WHOLE AIR FORCE CAREER.

———

During his final press conference as the Air Force Academy football coach, Fisher DeBerry spoke on behalf of himself and his wife, Lu Ann: "I pray we have made a difference in the lives of the ones who have been entrusted to us, and I hope we have honored Him in all we have tried to do."

Trust me, Coach, you did.

Coach DeBerry found me during a recruiting visit to Mississippi in 1982, after I had been rejected by most major colleges as a player who was a step too slow or not quite big enough to play on the Division I-A level. He gave me an opportunity to live my dream, and when I arrived in Colorado Springs, I found a group of young men just like me who were willing to pay any price to play for the Falcons. There was real genius in Coach DeBerry's approach to building a football program. He took young men who were not heavily recruited, brought them together and built them into a force much more powerful than the sum of the individual parts.

The foundation of the program was built on undying commitment to each other, as well as sacrifice, hard work, accountability and faith that we could accomplish our dreams. We adopted the identity of the fighting falcon, a powerful, fearless bird known to kill prey twice its size, and followed the vision of our leader, who expected to win. Coach DeBerry worked tirelessly and earned the respect of his players by serving them and offering each, from least to greatest, a full measure of dignity and respect.

As my wife, Aimee, and I teach our four young children the lessons of life, I often teach from my experiences at Air Force as a player and a coach. My kids know that quitting in life is never an option and that the 1986 Falcons of my senior season kept fighting to earn a 45-35 victory over Utah in Salt Lake City, even when we were down by 21 points at halftime. My kids know that Coach DeBerry, as a caring leader, visited my father, Bubba, in his Mississippi hospital room and visited my mother, Sheila, to offer encouragement during a particularly difficult time in our family. My kids watch us as parents do what Coach DeBerry told his young men to do each Sunday: "Go to church and call your mother and father and tell 'em how much you love 'em."

I recently gave a young man some advice straight from the mouth of Coach DeBerry. This young man told me that he was eager to meet that special someone. I told him, just like Coach DeBerry told me, "Never worry about finding the right girl to marry, because she will find you." The words brought a big smile to the young man's face.

Now as a leader in my company — I am an area director for Bristol-Myers Squibb — I often discuss the importance of executing aggressive fundamentals, like blocking and tackling, and remind others that although we can never be perfect, our effort will be. I encourage others with such phrases as "A champion is the one who gets up one more time than he is knocked down;" "It's easier to pull a rope than to push one;" "The only rule we have is to do what's right;" "There is no letter I in team." I was taught all of that while proudly playing for Air Force. Coach DeBerry showed his players how to win by deflecting praise to others and how to lose by taking complete responsibility. These many lessons have served me well during my career.

Coach DeBerry could have taken numerous job offers at some of the most prestigious universities in the country during his tenure at Air Force, yet he stayed loyal to us because "once a Falcon, always a Falcon." During the twilight of his coaching career, he stood taller than I've ever seen him stand, because he never would bow his head when the going got tough — except to his Master, who gave him the courage to persevere in all circumstances with love and humility.

The success of the Air Force football program is an inspiring story and taught us all that, in Coach DeBerry's words, "There is no limit to what we can attain if we don't care who gets the credit." I am humbled to have played just a small part in Air Force football history and am forever grateful to Coach DeBerry and Mrs. DeBerry for giving me an opportunity to be a part of the Falcon family. I am so glad and thankful that I took the "road less traveled" to Colorado Springs, for "it has made all the difference."

CHAPTER EIGHT

LT. COL. TERRY MAKI (RET.)

———

Linebacker
Four-year letterman (1983–86)
Graduated in 1987
Hometown: Libby, Mont.
Resides now: Missoula, Mont.

———

TERRY'S PERFORMANCE AGAINST NOTRE DAME IN 1985 TELLS YOU JUST HOW AMAZING HE WAS. HE SET A SCHOOL RECORD WITH 30 TACKLES AND BLOCKED A FIELD GOAL LATE IN THE GAME THAT WE RETURNED FOR THE WINNING TOUCHDOWN. HE WAS AN ALL-AMERICAN IN 1986, HIS SENIOR SEASON, AND MIGHT HAVE BEEN THE BEST LINEBACKER IN AIR FORCE HISTORY. HE HAD THE RIGHT TEMPERAMENT AND TOUGHNESS TO PLAY A VERY RUGGED POSITION AT A HIGH LEVEL. TERRY WOULD HAVE BEEN AN NCAA CHAMPION IN WRESTLING IF I HADN'T TAKEN HIM TO PLAY IN THE HULA BOWL ALL-STAR GAME IN HAWAII AFTER HIS SENIOR SEASON. HE HAD WRESTLED IN THREE NATIONAL CHAMPIONSHIPS BEFORE HIS SENIOR YEAR. I'M SO PROUD OF HIS AIR FORCE CAREER AND ALL THE GREAT THINGS HE DID FOR OUR NATION WHILE ON ACTIVE DUTY. AND I'M

ESPECIALLY PLEASED THAT HE IS NOW COACHING HIGH SCHOOL FOOTBALL
BACK IN HIS HOME STATE OF MONTANA.

––––––––

The art of influence is such a powerful concept because when it comes right down
to it, it's all we really have in our relationships with our spouses, children and
friends. Influence means seeing what someone can be and helping him or her get
there. Influence is a powerfully positive force when correctly applied and based on
a genuine concern to do well.

My father, Terry Sr., is one of the greatest influencers of my life. He holds
a great value system predicated on hard, honest work. There were no free lunches
around our house growing up, but my dad also believed I had something more to
offer, something I didn't always realize. When I made mistakes or got off track, he
would help me see things in a way that would give me the encouragement to keep
trying and not give up.

Fisher DeBerry was a profoundly influential coach — in football and in
life. As an Air Force Academy player, I don't remember much about what he or
the other coaches said regarding X's and O's, but to this day I vividly remember
him urging us to commit ourselves to the team, to each other, to our faith, to our
families and to others who meant the most to us. He constantly told us to call our
parents and tell them we loved them and appreciated all they had done for us.

Through all the notoriety and fame he garnered as one of the most
successful football coaches in NCAA history, Fisher never lost his sense of
gratefulness. To me, gratitude is the cornerstone of his personality. Having a
grateful attitude for our talents and blessings and conveying that to everyone you
come in contact with is the single key to happiness and ultimate success. That is
what he taught me through his influence. He laid out his personal beliefs for us to
consider for our own lives, and he truly lived what he believed.

Another key factor that enabled Coach DeBerry to influence his players was
his genuine concern for our welfare. Of course he wanted us to learn to win, but
he always conveyed a deeper concern for our development as men, and leaders.
Playing football at Air Force was a phenomenal experience primarily because the
players were committed to excellence and the coaches were fully committed to the
players. Instinctively, I knew I was a small part of something great.

Being an Air Force Falcon is a lifelong club, not just a four-year stint of
membership. Countless players have recounted to me their visits to games as
alumni, not knowing if they would be remembered or accepted but instead being

welcomed with open arms by Coach DeBerry and his staff. Coach DeBerry would remember details about former Air Force players who were not even starters for him, such as their fathers' occupations or their hometowns. To me, that is what it takes to have real lifetime influence. You have to walk the walk and really learn to love those you are supposed to serve.

Playing linebacker at the Air Force Academy was an honor and a formative experience. Of course, nobody involved in our 1985 game against Notre Dame at Falcon Stadium will ever forget it. That year was my junior season, and we were rolling. When the first Saturday of October arrived, we were 4-0 and had won by scores of 48-6 (Texas-El Paso), 49-7 (at Wyoming), 59-17 (Rice) and 49-12 (at New Mexico). We knew that beating Notre Dame would put us on the national map.

I remember watching game films that week and thinking how great it would be to win and be 5-0. I hardly slept all week. On game day, everything we practiced and rehearsed would play out on the field of friendly strife. Falcon Stadium was packed with a record crowd of 52,153 fans. The game was nationally televised by ABC Sports. Bart Weiss, our senior quarterback, had the offense moving the ball well, and our defense was bending but not breaking, preventing long plays. When the fourth quarter arrived, the game was close, just as we had hoped. But late in the game, we were behind 15-13, and the Notre Dame offense was driving for more points to put us away.

Thankfully, with a huge play from noseguard Dick Clark, we were able to stop the Fighting Irish on third down and force them to attempt a 37-yard field goal. Kevin Martin and I had pressured the Notre Dame kicker, John Carney, throughout the game. On this particular attempt late in the game, Kevin and I overloaded the left tackle, Kevin taking his outside shoulder and me taking the inside route. As the ball was snapped and we moved forward, the tackle blocked out on Kevin. That left a large, gaping hole for me to blast through the Irish's protection. I blocked the field goal, and the ball went nearly straight up in the air. A.J. Scott, our premier strong safety and the fastest man on the field, caught the ball and returned it 77 yards for the winning touchdown. We won 21-15. We were 5-0. I was much more thrilled about blocking that field goal than I was about having made 30 tackles, an Air Force record.

After the game, Bruce Johnson, our beloved defensive coordinator, said, "You know there was divine intervention with that blocked kick. Maki could have blocked it, and Ziegler could have caught it, but instead it was A.J. who caught it. And he's the fastest guy on the field." John Ziegler was a great defensive tackle for us on that 12-1 team, but he wasn't fast.

Playing football for a team like Air Force was a dream of mine. I was a two-time state wrestling champion in Montana and was highly recruited to wrestle in college but hardly recruited for football outside the state. So when the opportunity to attend the Air Force Academy arrived, it became a dream come true. I wanted to be a dual-sport athlete in college, and Air Force offered the best opportunity to do so. Wayne Baughman, the great AFA wrestling coach, helped me get accepted to the Air Force Prep School. Coming from Libby, a small Montana town, to the Air Force Academy was a big adjustment. But the players and coaches helped to make me feel part of the team.

Playing on a real team of young men helped me learn the value of teamwork. As Coach DeBerry would often say, "There is no *I* in the letter team." He really brought out the teamwork quality in all of us. Though it sounds like a cliché, no amount of personal recognition can compensate for being part of a great team.

After my graduation, I was fortunate to serve as a special-tactics officer in the Air Force. My deployments included Panama, Desert Storm, Bosnia, Somalia, Enduring Freedom and Iraqi Freedom. The values of teamwork I learned while playing Air Force football for Coach DeBerry helped me immeasurably to train, motivate and lead young troops in combat operations.

At Coach DeBerry's tribute dinner in May 2007, after he had retired from coaching, he said something to the effect of, "It's not so much whether the boy quit us, but whether we quit the boy." That statement sums up the attitude we should all strive for as spouses, parents, mentors and friends.

I retired from active duty after 20 years and three months of proud service and now work for the Air Force Special Operations Command at the University of Montana, focusing on research in health and human performance. Coach DeBerry's influence inspired me to become a high school football coach. Coaching appeals to me because of coaches like Fisher DeBerry, who influenced my life so positively that I will always be indebted to him for his words of advice, encouragement and wisdom. He uses his influence to better his fellow man. What better words can be said?

CHAPTER NINE

MAJ. TIM CURRY

Cornerback
Three-year letterman (1996–98)
Graduated in 1999
Hometown: Seattle
Resides now: Las Vegas

YOU COULDN'T FIND MANY BETTER CORNERBACKS THAN TIM. HE WAS GREAT ON SPECIAL TEAMS, TOO. HE HAD FIVE INTERCEPTIONS AS A JUNIOR IN 1997 AND PLAYED JUST AS WELL AS A SENIOR ON OUR 12-1 TEAM OF 1998. HE SET AN AIR FORCE RECORD BY BLOCKING NINE KICKS IN HIS CAREER, INCLUDING FIVE IN 1997, AND PLAYED IN THE HULA BOWL ALL-STAR GAME IN HAWAII AFTER HIS SENIOR SEASON. HE ALWAYS CAME UP WITH A BIG PLAY IN THE BIG GAMES. TIM TOOK GREAT PRIDE IN BLOCKING KICKS, AND HIS BLOCK IN OVERTIME TO WIN THE SAN DIEGO STATE GAME IN 1997 WAS A THING OF BEAUTY. HE WANTED TO BE A TEAM LEADER, TO BE THE BEST IN THE CLASSROOM, TO BE A BROTHER TO HIS TEAMMATES. THAT IS WHY HE IS HAVING SUCH AN OUTSTANDING CAREER AS AN AIR FORCE PILOT.

As great a role model as Coach DeBerry was to his players, and continues to be, I don't think he will mind knowing that he is the runner-up in my book on how to best live your life.

My all-time role model is Jesus Christ. No one has had a bigger, better influence on my life than Jesus, whose message couldn't be simpler or more important: Love God and love others. Anyone who does that has my highest respect and admiration. Live your life by Jesus' example, and you will do just fine. I try to remember that every day as an active-duty Air Force officer and as a member of the Air Force Academy football family, cherished roles that I'm honored to have.

People with passion and integrity are people to emulate because they live as an example to others while making them feel valued and loved. Thankfully, every football coach I had from age 6 onward were those type of people — including Coach DeBerry, who was a blessing to play for and learn from.

I didn't exactly set the world of Air Force football on fire when I joined the Falcons in 1995 as a freshman from Seattle. I broke my back, so I didn't play that season. As a sophomore, I was only splitting the playing time at cornerback. I had to be patient and stay pointed in the right direction. I became a full-time starter in 1997, my junior year, when we went 10-3 and played in the Las Vegas Bowl.

I swallowed a bitter pill when Navy (20-17) and Army (23-7) swept us in 1996 during my sophomore year. That year, the Army game was played at West Point, and they had a packed house. As our time ran out, I heard the Army coaches shouting, "You Air Force Falcons don't deserve to be on the same field as the Black Knights of the Hudson!" They whipped us pretty good, but that's the last thing I needed to hear at that painful time. Jason Sanderson, one of our safeties and a classmate, also heard it. We looked at each other and instantly vowed that we'd never lose to Army again. And we didn't.

We swept Navy (10-7) and Army (24-0) the next year. In 1998, we followed up with another sweep: Navy (49-7) and Army (35-7). My final trip to West Point was the best. By halftime, the Army fans were silent. Early in the third quarter, they began leaving Michie Stadium. That's how big a blowout we enjoyed! This time I didn't hear anybody saying the Air Force Falcons didn't deserve to be on that field.

Coach DeBerry exhibited an unmatched energy level, so it was easy to play hard for him. He was much older than we were and still going a million miles per hour; how could any of his players ever feel tired? Coach DeBerry's nonstop energy, passion and dedication to living and playing football the right way motivated me to be all that I could be, on and off the field.

My Air Force teammates are an everlasting brotherhood. We've been there for each other on the field and in combat. I have had nine wonderful and exciting years in the active-duty Air Force, yet I haven't experienced the same camaraderie we had on our 12-1 football team my senior year at the academy. It's an unbreakable bond strengthened by teamwork, passion, dedication and hard work — the ingredients of a successful life.

My peers in the Air Force, especially my squadron members, are wonderful people, and our nation has every reason to be proud of them. They are men and women who treat one another with the utmost respect, dignity and professionalism as military warriors in very turbulent times in our country. The sacrifice each makes is worthy of a daily salute from American citizens.

When I was a cadet, I thought some of the stuff we had to memorize and the strictness of our day-to-day routine was pretty much ridiculous. Once I got into pilot training, I realized that what I had been taught in Colorado Springs was for a key reason. War is not fun and games, so you had better be prepared when it arrives.

I flew F-16 combat and combat-support missions during Operation Iraqi Freedom and Operation Enduring Freedom while stationed in Germany for three years. I was involved in Operation Iraqi Freedom from day one and remain extremely proud of my participation in those missions. We had a job to do, and we did it.

Now that I'm stationed at Nellis Air Force Base, I fly Unmanned Aerial System aircraft out at the Tonopah Test Range in Nevada. Working with such a high-tech system is extremely challenging. Yet it's also very rewarding knowing that I'm doing my part to help us win the war against terrorism.

I hope to emulate Coach DeBerry on the field this fall when I begin my own coaching career. I will be a volunteer special-teams coach for the Shadow Ridge High School football team in North Las Vegas and can't wait to get started. Volunteering is perfect because I don't need or want the paycheck. What I need is the opportunity to take part in the wonderful profession of coaching. If I can have the same positive impact on the lives of my players at Shadow Ridge that Coach DeBerry and his staff have had on my life, I know I will be a success as a coach.

Coach DeBerry once asked me a question that sticks with me today: "What do you want people to say about you when you are gone?" I was an Air Force cadet at the time and playing cornerback for the Falcons, so he probably was talking to me in that context. Nevertheless, you and I can apply this question to ourselves today. When it's all said and done with Tim Curry, I hope people will say that I lived my life trying to be like Jesus, seeking to love Him and love others. How do you want others to remember you?

Chapter Ten

STEED LOBOTZKE

Offensive tackle
Two-year letterman (1990–91)
Graduated in 1992
Hometown: Roseville, Calif.
Resides now: Winston-Salem, N.C.

STEED WAS A REAL STUDENT OF THE GAME WHEN HE PLAYED ON THE OFFENSIVE LINE FOR THE FALCONS, AND HE STILL IS AS A MEMBER OF THE WAKE FOREST COACHING STAFF. HE WAS SELECTED TO THE ALL-WESTERN ATHLETIC CONFERENCE FIRST TEAM AS A SENIOR IN 1991, THE YEAR WE BEAT MISSISSIPPI STATE IN THE LIBERTY BOWL TO COMPLETE A 10-3 SEASON. STEED DEVELOPED HIMSELF INTO A GREAT PLAYER THROUGH GOOD OLD-FASHIONED HARD WORK AND COMMITMENT. STEED WAS A VERY CONSISTENT PLAYER, WEEK IN AND WEEK OUT. THAT IS WHY HE IS ONE OF THE BRIGHT, YOUNG SUPERSTAR COACHES IN THE NCAA TODAY AT WAKE FOREST. I TRIED TO CONVINCE HIM NOT TO COACH BUT TO GO INTO THE CORPORATE WORLD BECAUSE HE IS SO SMART. I'M GLAD

HE DIDN'T LISTEN TO ME, BECAUSE HE IS SUCH A POWERFUL INFLUENCE TODAY ON SO MANY YOUNG PLAYERS.

———

The Air Force Academy is not a college. The purpose of the academy is to produce military officers, hardened soldiers ready for war. To harden its soldiers, the institution itself must also be hard. The academy is hard in so many ways, you almost can't list them all. You are put through endless varieties of military training. You are buried under an avalanche of brutal academic classes. You are pushed to the limit in every way imaginable.

Football was my only refuge. Practices were tough and time consuming, but I loved it so much that I didn't even notice the hardships compared with the other parts of my day. Football was the best part of my day and provided all my best memories. For this reason, I was inspired to become a football coach.

My father was vice president of a bank. I have a degree in economics. I believed I was going to follow his footsteps into the world of high finance, but my academy experience taught me to follow my heart rather than my wallet. Coincidentally, my father had been saying the same thing for years, but some lessons need to be learned firsthand.

Now that I am in the coaching profession, as the offensive line coach and offensive coordinator at Wake Forest University, I cannot help but compare my job to being a cadet. The most relevant comparison is that I have 25 hours of work to do and only a 24-hour day! I am exaggerating, of course, but the academy forces you to be organized, use your time wisely, prioritize your tasks — and work fast.

At the academy, you cannot possibly get everything done that's demanded of you; you survive by doing what really matters. I use these skills during our in-season weekly schedule to check our previous game; investigate our next opponent; identify game-plan personnel; determine formation, shift, motion and play design; schedule practices; teach linemen; and call plays to win a football game. Anytime I begin to think that my job is too tough, I remind myself that the absolute hardest day as a coach is still easier than just being at the academy — and then I get back to work with a smile.

Our football team at Air Force practiced hard, but we rarely practiced long, especially on days with classes. Coach DeBerry knew what a precious commodity time was for cadets. When we got to practice, we flew from drill to drill. Set up fast, get what work you need and get on to the next drill. Maximize the number of practice reps for everyone, and "coach on the run."

The linebackers coach during my years at the academy was Jim Grobe. Now Jim is my boss and the head coach at Wake Forest. We model our practices after this effective style: Get in, go hard, and get out.

Like many others, I relished the role of underdog while playing at Air Force. Every week was the same story: We were too small and slow to win. The amazing thing was, we never believed it no matter how often we read it. That optimistic attitude started with the coaching staff. You never sensed defeatism or desperation from our coaches at Air Force. On the contrary, you sensed that they expected to win.

Nowhere was this more evident than in the offensive-line meeting room. Our coach was Bob Noblitt. Despite his diminutive stature and balding head, we lived in fear of him. Not that he would hurt us or even yell at us; we just did not want to disappoint him. I knew he expected us to win, so I did everything in my power to meet his expectations. Players only play this way if they believe the coaches care and that everybody is in it together. Coach DeBerry and his whole staff did a phenomenal job of creating that environment.

I have tried to bring this attitude to my players now even though Wake Forest has had a checkered football past. I don't *think* they can win, I *expect* them to win, and I hope they believe my expectations and are inspired enough to make them a reality. Wake Forest expecting to win helped us win the Atlantic Coast Conference championship in 2006 and play in the Orange Bowl that season.

For the longest time, winning on the field was my only goal, and it was completely disconnected from my off-the-field conduct. Playing for Coach DeBerry taught me otherwise. You can't show poor character off the field all week in your classes and squadron and then flip some switch in the fourth quarter of the big game and win in the end by overcoming exhaustion and adversity with exceptional character. If you want to be a rock-solid teammate and player on game day, you have to be a rock-solid person every day.

I don't think all college football programs teach that philosophy, but I am so thankful Coach DeBerry beat it into us every time he spoke. He did it straightforward by calling us out. He did it with down-home stories. He injected the morals through a thousand corny sayings and slogans, which came to be known affectionately as "DeBerryisms." But no matter what he was saying, it always came back to our one-and-only team rule: Do the right thing. And it worked because he didn't just preach it; he lived it.

Following my graduation, I was fortunate enough to be picked as a graduate assistant for the Air Force football team. My job was to assist the offensive coaching staff over the next year. It was June, supposedly a quiet time for a football coach — but not at Air Force. Coach DeBerry called the offensive staff together for a week of meetings all day, every day, and the Falcons weren't changing anything from the previous year or even looking at their upcoming opponents! I could not imagine what we were going to talk about.

Coach DeBerry asked each offensive coach to show the other coaches how he taught every aspect of every position for every play. I watched DeBerry, the record-setting national coach of the year, sitting there taking notes and asking questions about where on the ball the center put his thumb while snapping it to the quarterback. Being young and a new coach, I didn't get it at first. What could the great Coach DeBerry possibly be getting out of this? But as I watched, I realized that it just burned in him to be the best football coach he could possibly be, and no matter how many Commander-in-Chief's trophies for service-academy dominance he brought home, he never had all the answers, and he could always learn some little tidbit to make himself better.

I haven't stopped studying the game since that moment. Thanks, Coach DeBerry.

CHAPTER ELEVEN

SCOTT McKAY

———

Halfback
Three-year letterman (1998–2000)
Graduated in 2001
Hometown: Santa Clara, Calif.
Resides now: New York City

———

S COTTY MADE SUCH A POSITIVE IMPRESSION ON HIS TEAMMATES, HE
WAS VOTED OUR TEAM MVP AS A JUNIOR EVEN THOUGH HE DIDN'T
LEAD THAT 1999 TEAM IN RUSHING. HE WENT OUT IN STYLE A YEAR LATER
WHEN HE HELPED US GO 9-3 IN HIS SENIOR SEASON, INCLUDING A VICTORY
OVER FRESNO STATE IN THE SILICON VALLEY BOWL. SCOTTY WAS TOO
SMALL TO PLAY AT THE DIVISION I-A LEVEL, BUT HE DIDN'T KNOW THAT.
HE WAS ANOTHER GIANT OF A PLAYER AND COULD DO SO MANY THINGS
WITH THE BALL. I LOVED BEING AROUND HIM BECAUSE SCOTTY WAS ONE OF
THE FEW PLAYERS SHORTER THAN I. JOKING ASIDE, SCOTTY COULD REALLY
BRIGHTEN YOUR DAY BECAUSE HE NEVER ALLOWED HIMSELF TO GET DOWN
ABOUT ANYTHING. HE LOVED TO COME TO PRACTICE AND GO TO WORK TO

GET BETTER, AND WHAT A JOY HE WAS TO COACH. HE BELIEVED HE COULD
SCORE EVERY TIME HE HAD THE BALL.

––––––––

Not only do you learn the importance of teamwork at the Air Force
Academy; you learn the all-important lessons of how to handle adversity in
a professional manner. All cadets quickly discover that adversity is a daily
occurrence. Whether you are facing an important academic test or a superior
you dislike, whether you are getting yelled at or physically challenged as a
freshman, whether you are involved in a leadership challenge with your peers,
the Air Force Academy tests your ability to manage stress and adversity every
day of your enrollment.

I handled adversity and stress by taking a long-term view of a situation and
trying to focus on the positive aspects of my life. I learned to surround myself
with good-natured people who had a positive outlook on life. I was very fortunate
to surround myself with some amazing people as a cadet, people who took a
proactive interest in seeing that I was successful not only in the classroom and on
the football field but also in life.

Ask me to list the people at Air Force who had the most positive influence
on me, and I struggle with that, simply because there are too many to count. But I
will try, because the significant roles they played in shaping my life deserve a salute
and define the power of influence this book is based on.

In academics, my top influencers were Dr. Kurt Heppard and Dr.
Steve Green of the Air Force Academy management department. I spent a
considerable amount of time with these two amazing professors, learning from
them not only in the classroom but also learning how to make an impact in life.
They maintained a unique, positive and long-term view on how the academy
shapes young people to be great leaders. While I was on active duty, I came
back to the academy to speak to their classes and talk about how the academy
prepared me for life as an officer and to perform my daily responsibilities
successfully. To this day, we keep in touch, and I consider them two of my
closest business and professional mentors.

In athletics, I remember Russ Laney, Tony Peck and Richard Bell with
great fondness. At the time, Russ was an assistant athletic director. Tony was
our football team's terrific head trainer. Coach Bell was the assistant on Fisher
DeBerry's staff who recruited me to Air Force in 1996. I am blessed to know them
all. One of the best aspects of playing football at the academy is the great people

you meet within the athletic department and within the Colorado Springs and Denver communities.

Russ ran the sponsorship and marketing aspects of the athletic department while I was a player. He traveled to all the games, and I watched him interact with the boosters and dignitaries who always seemed to be around the football program. Russ liked to introduce me as "Scotty McKay, pound for pound the best college football player in the country." Though probably not entirely true – I was listed as being 5 feet 8 inches tall and weighing 175 pounds in 2000, my senior season – I was fortunate to learn how to interact and communicate with business, community and military leaders across the country with Russ' help. Russ also stressed to me the importance of "making the people around you better." I can't think of a better life mission than of service and care for others. Russ and I remain good friends and talk on a regular basis.

Considering that I was an undersized running back playing major college football, I spent a lot of time with Tony and the other trainers. Tony always called me "Tiny Falcon." That started after a newspaper article was published about me in the Colorado Springs Gazette with this headline: "Tiny Falcon makes significant contribution." The morning it appeared in The Gazette, that article was posted above the taping station where Tony worked on my ankles and occasional injuries. I shared with Tony about how the season was going, about academy issues and about how to handle team issues from a leadership perspective. As a team leader, I frequently confided in Tony and asked for his advice on how to handle team issues. Tony taught me an aggressive and compassionate leadership style that I utilize today in my daily interaction with junior bankers in my post-Air Force career as an investment banker in New York City.

Outside of my family, Coach Bell had the greatest influence on my young-adult life. I hold the highest respect for Coach Bell and everything he did for me personally, athletically and professionally. I'll never forget the first time we met on a rainy winter day at my high school in the San Jose area, where he greeted me with his strong Southern accent. I think Coach Bell expected me to be a little bit bigger than I was, after watching my highlight and game films. We had a great talk about the Air Force Academy and built a strong friendship right there. Coach Bell took a chance recruiting me. He was the only coach who believed I could play and be successful at the major college level. Even my own high school coach didn't believe it.

Not only did Coach Bell recruit me to Air Force; he helped keep me there when I was homesick and ready to return to California. Coach Bell taught me how to handle personal and team situations the right way, and he made me a better person. I felt like he treated me and loved me like a son, and I respected and treated him as if he were my father. Coach Bell and my relationship with him is a great tribute to Coach DeBerry and the type of staff members he surrounded himself with to build such a great football program. Coach DeBerry brought in coaches, like Richard Bell, who were great men and built longevity at Air Force because they believed in the mission of the academy and the players they coached.

More than anyone else, though, I consider my father, mother and younger brother as the people who have had the greatest impact on my life. My parents, Marty and Dianne McKay, raised me to feel good about the person I am. They parented me when I required it and were best friends when I needed a friend. They taught me priorities and how to achieve my ambitious goals. They never suppressed my competitive, determined and active spirit and also made a point to celebrate my successes and those of my brother Bryan.

When I left home, Coach DeBerry and his staff of assistants essentially became extensions of my parents. The same wonderful style of parenting I received as a child, I received from Coach DeBerry and his staff while I was an Air Force cadet. No wonder the Falcons were so successful during the DeBerry era.

More than a decade after I played for the Falcons, Air Force football continues to have a strong, positive impact on my life. Falcon football taught me how to win and be successful at a very competitive level when our competition looked better on paper. I applied this lesson when I interviewed for my current job on Wall Street. There were more qualified candidates who came from a higher ranked business school, and had more applicable work experience, or whose fathers were clients of the firm. I relied solely on my competitiveness, determination and work ethic, all honed at the Air Force Academy, and was hired by a great firm for the position I wanted. There is no situation in which I feel I can't be successful, simply because of the success the Air Force football team had while I played for Coach DeBerry.

Playing for the Falcons also taught me the importance of family. I learned the importance of a successful marriage and family by witnessing the success of Coach DeBerry and his family and the staff members and their families. It's all about honesty, love and patience. Coach DeBerry preached family values nonstop. He treated the team as his family and the players as his sons. The coaches would often bring the players into their homes for dinner and talk about life outside of football. This reinforced Coach DeBerry's strong message about the importance of family and not letting your brothers (your teammates) down.

Nobody ever plays for the Falcons and forgets the games after they graduate. I still vividly remember almost all of our games. Here are some that continue to stand out in my mind:

- 1998 vs. Colorado State: My sophomore season, the year the Falcons went 12-1 and won the Western Athletic Conference championship. We beat CSU 30-27 at Falcon Stadium early in the season after we trailed at halftime by 17 points. We won the game on a last-second field goal. It was the first and last time I was ever on a team that won a game after trailing by such a huge margin at halftime.

- 1998 vs. Rice: We needed to beat the Owls at Falcon Stadium to represent our division in the WAC championship game in Las Vegas. It wasn't going our way until Mike Tyler, who was playing with a torn knee ligament, intercepted a pass and returned it for a touchdown. We won 22-16. Mike's great courage that day remains a tribute to the type of player Air Force has and how perseverance can lead to amazing results.

- 1998 vs. Brigham Young: We played the powerhouse Cougars in the WAC championship game and came from behind to win 20-13, stretching our record that year to 11-1. It ended up being Coach DeBerry's only outright WAC championship.

- 1998 vs. Washington: The Falcons accepted an invitation to play the Huskies in the Oahu Bowl in Honolulu. I scored two touchdowns — one on a 15-yard run; the other on a 30-yard reception — to help us win 45-25. That was the point in my Air Force football career that I believed I became a "go-to" player and felt comfortable with my role in our triple-option offense. And what a thrill it was to see our seniors go out as winners, with a rout of a Pac-10 power program.

- 1999 vs. New Mexico: One of our few losses I remember in detail. It was my junior season, and we started out with sky-high expectations after going 12-1 the year before. But we finished 6-5, with no bowl game to play. We closed that disappointing season with a 33-28 loss at New Mexico, a team we should have beaten. What made that loss especially painful was that we played uninspired football in our seniors' last game. I vowed never to let that happen to me and the seniors in my class the following year.

- 2000 vs. San Diego State: My last game at Falcon Stadium. We beat the Aztecs 45-24 on a cold, sunny Saturday afternoon in mid-November. I remember all the emotion I was feeling while standing on our sideline after Coach DeBerry pulled the starters to get the backups some playing time in the fourth quarter. I reflected on all my years at the academy, all the highs and lows. Coach DeBerry saw that I had tears of joy in my eyes. He gave me a bear hug and several pats on the back. Looking me straight in the eyes, he simply said, "Thank you." I still get pretty emotional thinking about that. It just goes to show you how important Air Force football is to the players and coaches in that program. Two words at just the right time summed up all the sacrifices, the emotions, the challenges, the friendships, the wins and losses. To this day, I prefer to decline invitations to watch the Falcons play from a spot on their sideline so I don't ever dilute that special moment I shared with Coach DeBerry that afternoon of my final home game.
- 2000 vs. Fresno State: My last football game, the Silicon Valley Bowl. We played the Bulldogs in San Jose, in the San Jose State Spartan Stadium. More than 150 family members and friends came to watch me. We won a 37-34 shoot-out to complete a 9-3 season, beating a tough Fresno State team that was quarterbacked by David Carr, who would become the No. 1 pick in the NFL draft in 2002. As for me, my football career had come full circle. I could not have asked for a better opportunity or outcome.

I'll always remember celebrating our success with my teammates and coaches. We traveled to the White House to meet President Bush and celebrate our Commander-in-Chief's Trophy. The following year, after 9/11, I would make the trip to Washington again, this time as an Air Force assistant coach. I'll always remember Coach DeBerry and his leadership, conviction, passion and love for the Air Force Academy, the football team, his players and his staff.

There are two things he said to the team and one thing he said to me personally that stayed with me long after my last game:

- "Don't let your brother down." By this, Coach DeBerry meant to not do anything that would bring shame to your teammates, the coaching staff and the football program, and also to limit your mental mistakes on the field.
- "If you see a turtle sitting on a fence post, you know he didn't get there by himself." This is probably my favorite "DeBerryism." Coach twisted the English language in a wonderful way and used analogies that required us to interpret exactly what he meant. This saying meant that we've all achieved

success by various measures, but nobody has ever done it all by himself. I always try to recognize and thank the people who have helped me along the way, no matter how small or great their contributions.

- Finally, Coach DeBerry challenged me in ways that no other coach could. When I was attending the Air Force Prep School, I seriously considered leaving and returning to California. Coach DeBerry convinced me to stick it out and give my freshman year at the academy a shot.

One year later, I was a freshman cadet at the Academy. I was lifting weights with a teammate who had attended the prep school with me, when Coach DeBerry came up to the two of us and said, "I'm not sure which one of you is going to stay at the academy. But Scotty, if I was a betting man, I sure wouldn't put my money on you." From that moment on, I never considered leaving the Air Force Academy. I was so motivated to prove Coach DeBerry wrong and be a successful player and leader on the team, I focused intensely on making that goal a reality. To this day, I am so grateful that Coach DeBerry decided to say those words to me.

CHAPTER TWELVE

JOE WOOD

———

Kicker
Three-year letterman (1989–91)
Graduated in 1992
Hometown: Mission Viejo, Calif.
Resides now: Ladera Ranch, Calif.

———

JOE'S WORK ETHIC WAS AS STRONG AS HIS KICKING LEG, AND HE WAS A BOOMER AS A KICKER. HE KICKED 39 FIELD GOALS FOR THE FALCONS FROM 1989–91, WHEN HE WAS ONE OF THE BEST PLAYERS IN THE WESTERN ATHLETIC CONFERENCE AT HIS POSITION, AND HAD ENOUGH TALENT TO BE SELECTED IN THE NFL DRAFT. HE KICKED A 46-YARD FIELD GOAL LATE IN THE FOURTH QUARTER OF OUR LIBERTY BOWL UPSET OF OHIO STATE IN 1990. ONCE WE GOT SMART AS A COACHING STAFF AND MADE JOE A FULL-TIME KICKER, HE BECAME AS GOOD A KICKER AS THERE WAS IN THE COUNTRY. I NEVER DOUBTED HE WOULD GET US POINTS. I GUESS THE PROS FELT THAT WAY ALSO, OR HE WOULDN'T HAVE BEEN DRAFTED. HIS KICKING RHYTHM WAS POETRY IN ACTION.

———

When I told my father that a football coach from the Air Force Academy came to talk to me, he almost lost it. He knew exactly what a degree from a military academy could do for me. My father tried to guide me to what he knew would be one of the best decisions I ever made. He used subtle hints like "It's your decision, but if you don't go to the academy, it will be one of the worst decisions you will ever make." Well, the hints worked, and I decided to go to Air Force. I went there not really knowing what I was getting into. I knew it was a great education, was prestigious, had an NCAA Division I-A football team and could lead to a career as a pilot. I figured I played sports all my life, had good grades and came from a disciplined family.

I was not ready for my freshman year at the base of the breathtaking Rampart Range. The academic load, military responsibilities, freshman-year rigors and homesickness overwhelmed me. Air Force football was the one thing that kept many of us from going insane.

My freshman year would have been much more difficult without being able to go down to the Cadet Field House, work out, practice or just blow off some steam. Whether it was actual preparation for football, just messing around with friends or telling each other freshman-year war stories, it was a welcome break from the reality of what was waiting for us up on "the hill." To be totally honest, I found camaraderie on the football team that I didn't feel up on the hill. Not to say there weren't some great young men and women at the academy. I probably met some of the best and smartest people I will ever meet in my life there. But I never felt the unity anywhere else that I felt with the fellas down on the field.

All the varsity athletes tended to gravitate toward each other, but especially the football team. I knew the upperclassmen on the team would always be looking out for me, and it never would get to where I couldn't handle it up on the hill. They did it for me and I, in turn, helped the freshmen when I was an upperclassman. Coach DeBerry and his staff were a big part of the unity our team had. It was many things, such as Coach DeBerry saying, "Take care of one another when you are up on the hill" or "Hug your brother" after a win or a loss. The coaches often opened their houses to players for weekend barbecues, naps or to just hang out. We were a family.

My football and cadet career didn't exactly start out on the best note. I came into the academy standing 6 feet 2 inches and weighing 210 pounds. I felt I probably needed to get to 230 pounds to give myself a shot at playing linebacker. After basic cadet training, I weighed only 179. My dreams of being a Division I-A linebacker were slipping away. I approached Coach Johnson, who told me to play wide receiver until I got my weight back up. I did and played

OK for the time being, but I didn't really have Division I-A speed for a wide receiver. However, I knew I could kick a football.

I had practiced countless hours with my father and at one point felt pretty confident about getting a scholarship as a kicker. I kicked in two games in high school but was out the rest of my senior season because of a groin pull. I could play linebacker and receiver but couldn't kick. The kicking motion hurt too much. About two weeks into my freshman season at Air Force, I decided to split my time playing offense and kicking. It turned out to be a great decision. I ended up doing much more for our team as a kicker than I ever would have as a linebacker.

To add to my rocky start in football, one night, four other football players and I decided to blow off some steam. The academy's wing commander wouldn't allow any freshmen to have a pass off the base. We walked off the base without permission, got beer and brought it back to the field house. Of course, we got caught. We were facing a pretty big punishment on the hill, but we were more worried about what Coach DeBerry was going to do if he found out. We went to an upperclassman for advice.

Troy Calhoun, Air Force's current head coach and an AFA senior at the time, told us we needed to tell Coach DeBerry, which we did. We quickly learned what Coach DeBerry thought of players who thought of themselves before they thought of the team. We ran every day after practice with Coach DeBerry or one of the assistant coaches. From that point on, I did a pretty good job of staying out of trouble.

Coach DeBerry surrounded himself with a great bunch of coaches over the years. Coaching at a military academy is one of the more challenging jobs you can find. Your talent pool probably isn't more than 10 percent of what most schools have to draw from because of the high academic standards and the military commitment. Yet our coaches were able to maximize each player's ability. My senior season, we ended up ranked 24th in the nation. We won the Liberty Bowl for the second straight year and finished 10-3. Not bad for a bunch of little guys with no speed.

Many games still stick out in my mind. Games against Army and Navy, our rivals. Games against Mississippi State, Ole Miss, Brigham Young and Colorado State. But no games bring back fonder memories than our Liberty Bowl victory over Ohio State in 1990 and playing Notre Dame. J.T. Tokish, a teammate and now the Falcons' team doctor, said it best when he said our team was comprised of guys who were told they weren't big enough or fast enough. It was the truth. We had a lot to prove every time we took to the field, especially against teams of Ohio State's and Notre Dame's caliber. Both teams were supposed to kill us, but Coach DeBerry's teams always played exceptionally well as underdogs. The coaches did a pretty good job of getting us up for most games. We never were big enough to take any opponent for granted, but I always remember our team being especially fired up to play the better teams.

Ohio State had lost to Michigan in 1990 in the final quarter, but the Buckeyes believed they should have won. Had they beat Michigan, they would have played in the Rose Bowl. That is the dream of any Big Ten or Pac-10 player. We had to win a game against Texas-El Paso in the final quarter just to make it to a bowl game. We did it, beating the Miners 14-13 in El Paso, and brought a 6-5 record to the Liberty Bowl my junior season. The Buckeyes, meanwhile, felt they deserved better. For weeks, newspaper articles talked about how great Ohio State was and how Air Force stood no chance against the Buckeyes in Memphis. I remember one Ohio State player being interviewed on TV. He said the Buckeyes planned to run up the score on us to prove they belonged in the Rose Bowl. No one even considered the fight in the team that was preparing to line up against them.

We were excited about the challenge. Our defense stepped up, and our offense played well enough to seal the victory. Our defense held Ohio State to 11 points and even scored a touchdown. We won 23-11. The score didn't really reflect the game. We kicked the Buckeyes' butts. A couple turnovers by us that negated long drives and a snap that went over our punter's head for a safety kept Ohio State in the game. The interception that Carlton McDonald, our All-American cornerback, returned 40 yards for a touchdown in the fourth quarter to seal it ranks as the best memory of my Air Force football career.

Then there was Notre Dame, who in the 1990s was as dominant as USC is now. I think the Fighting Irish were ranked No. 1 in the nation two of the four years we played them when I was at Air Force. Notre Dame players from these teams loaded the NFL draft: Tony Rice, Michael Stonebreaker, Rick Mirer, Jerome Bettis, Todd Lyght, Ricky Watters, Rocket Ismail, Chris Zorich and Bryant Young, to name just a few.

Our Notre Dame games were particularly special for me because my father grew up in Gary, Ind., which is near South Bend, and was a huge Notre Dame fan. We never beat the Irish when I was at Air Force, but we always played them tough. During my brief time in the NFL, I talk to several players from Notre Dame. All of them told me about the respect they had for the military academies and how we always played hard to the last whistle. A defensive back from Notre Dame told me that our fullback, Jason Jones, hit him harder than he had ever been hit before. He said he got up seeing stars after that collision.

Coach DeBerry's teams were well respected across the nation. This became evident to me whenever I had the opportunity to meet other coaches, players and fans. I had the pleasure of meeting many coaches and players when I played in the Japan Bowl all-star game and in my travels in the NFL and World League. Johnny Majors of Tennessee, R.C. Slocum from Texas A&M, longtime NFL coach Dan Reeves, Heisman Trophy winner Ty Detmer from BYU, and Craig Hentrich of Notre Dame all had stories about watching us play or playing against us. They always mentioned how tough our players were, how disciplined we were and how they liked watching the underdogs win yet again. I even had a fanatic Michigan graduate give me a hug for being on the Air Force team that beat Ohio State!

Not only did Coach DeBerry and his staff prepare us for football; they did it the right way. I was raised as a Christian, but I never considered myself ultra religious. Even people with no religion in their lives would have been impressed to see how Fisher DeBerry led his life while coaching the Falcons. Coach DeBerry always emphasized the importance of thinking of your family and thanking God for our many blessings. Anyone who has known Coach DeBerry knows how true to his family and religion he is. He consistently reminded us that football is a small part of what life is all about. And he was right. It took growing up and having a family of my own for much of that message to really hit home.

There is another story I love telling that shows how straight-laced Fisher DeBerry was as coach of the Falcons. My sophomore year, we were down in Fort Worth playing Texas Christian as a rare heavy favorite. We were coming off a loss to top-ranked Notre Dame the week before, and we were going to use a win over TCU to get us back on track in our push to win the Western Athletic Conference title. Instead, we came out as flat as I have ever seen an Air Force team. We came into halftime down and knew we were about to get an earful from the coaching staff. We all waited by our lockers for the coaches to come into the room. The door flew open, and Coach DeBerry came running in. He took his hat off and slammed it to the ground. Then he yelled, "Gentlemen, excuse my language.

But gosh darn it; you are playing like horse manure!" That was classic Fisher DeBerry. Good thing he warned us it was coming.

I use the tools I learned at Air Force in everything I do. I wasn't aware of all the things I was picking up along the way, but things I take for granted now may not have been so easy. The discipline, public speaking and work ethic I learned at Air Force help me tremendously in civilian life. I have been in sales since I stopped kicking a football. I'm now a vice president for the largest surplus lines insurance brokerage in the nation. My current career is something I attribute to my academy relationships. I was given my first interview through the introduction and recommendation of another Air Force graduate and football player. There are top-notch Air Force Academy graduates across this great country. They have opened doors I never might have gone through without their help and guidance.

Someday, I hope my sons will be lucky enough to attend a great school and play for a coach like Coach DeBerry. But I hope their story is a bit different than mine. One kicker in the family is enough. I want them to be inside linebackers.

CHAPTER THIRTEEN

CHUCK PETERSEN

Defensive back
Four-year letterman (1980–83)
Graduated in 1985
Junior-varsity offensive coordinator (1990)
Varsity receivers coach (1991–96)
Quarterbacks and fullbacks coach (1997–2006)
Offensive coordinator (2000–06)
Hometown: Fort Worth, Texas
Resides now: Denton, Texas

CHUCK IS AN EXAMPLE OF A GOOD COLLEGE PLAYER WHO BECAME A GREAT COLLEGE COACH BECAUSE HE KNEW HOW TO WORK. CHUCK WAS A VERY SMART PLAYER FOR THE FALCONS, ALWAYS IN THE RIGHT POSITION. HE IS A VERY SMART COACH WHO HAD A GREAT BELIEF AND UNDERSTANDING OF OUR SYSTEM. HE CALLED SOME GREAT GAMES AND WINS DURING HIS LONG TENURE ON THE AIR FORCE STAFF. CHUCK HAS ALL THE CREDENTIALS TO BE AN OUTSTANDING HEAD COACH SOMEDAY.

When I was asked by Coach DeBerry to write a chapter for his book, I was honored and somewhat overwhelmed. I have been influenced over the years by great men in all areas of my life, and it's difficult to give credit to all those who have made a difference in my life. I am the man I am today, like it or not, because of these men.

The man who has shaped me the most is my father, Chuck Petersen. Although coaching isn't his profession, he has been and continues to be the most important coach in my life. For 45 years, he has modeled for me how to be a great husband and father. Coaching is what I do, now as an assistant at the University of North Texas in Denton, but being a husband and father is who I am, and these are my most important roles.

My first two youth football coaches, John Roberts and Bob Frazier, were critical to shaping me. Both volunteered to coach even though they didn't have sons on the team. They showed me what service to others truly meant. These men also fueled my passion to play football, made the game fun and taught me the fundamentals that carried me throughout my career.

My next great coaching influence was Ken Hatfield, my head coach at the Air Force Academy. I am a coach today because of him. First, he showed me that you can coach hard, tough and passionately but still be the man God calls you to be. He was also my first real Christian influence outside the home. He wasn't afraid of who he was and lived his faith every day.

Col. Neal Wolfard, now retired, was the greatest leader I have had the privilege of working with. As my commander during my first Air Force assignment, he was tough, honest and fair. He had unbelievable integrity in everything he did. He preached to all of us that the mission came first, but he understood that the people who accomplished the mission were critical. Col. Wolfard took care of his people better than anyone I have been around. He would have been a great coach, and I am thankful for his help in my development.

Last, but certainly not least, comes Fisher DeBerry. I was blessed to be a part of his staff for 17 years at Air Force, and most of who I am as a coach, a father and a husband comes from him. During our many talks, he stressed the importance of controlling the things you can control. Many things occur in football and in life that we have no control over; the key to success is to maximize your efforts on the things you can control.

Ironically, the most important lesson I learned from Coach DeBerry came during our last couple of weeks together at Air Force. It wasn't a good time for anyone associated with the great program he developed; he was being attacked personally and professionally from those on the outside and the inside. He was treated very poorly and in the end was told to make some decisions he wasn't comfortable making. He handled the situation with unbelievable class and dignity. As much as he hurt, he put the football program and the institution above his own feelings. He modeled Jesus during that moment of crisis more than anyone I ever witnessed.

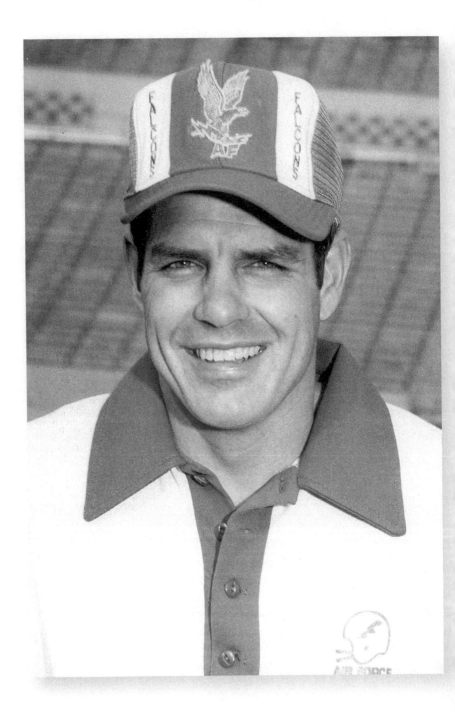

Chapter Fourteen

Ken Hatfield

———

Head coach (1979–83)
Offensive coordinator (1978)
Hometown: Helena, Ark.
Resides now: Springdale, Ark.

———

Kenny was the Air Force head coach who brought me to the academy as an assistant in 1980. He was the national coach of the year in 1983, when the Falcons finished 10-2, and was also a great head coach at Arkansas, Clemson and Rice after leaving the academy. He's one of the most inspirational people in my life. Kenny will go down as one of the best to have ever coached the game. He was a master at getting players to believe. I always have said that Ben Martin was the father of Air Force football, but Kenny was responsible for getting Air Force football back to national prominence and to the level of prestige the program enjoys today. Kenny was a great builder of men, socially, athletically, academically and spiritually, which I believe is the purpose of the academy.

———

The Fighting Falcons of Air Force football truly fulfill the mission of the Air Force Academy, which first and foremost is to train leaders. To be competitive against other major college teams loaded with players who aspire to play professional football, Air Force players accept the challenge of the time-consuming academy life and balance that with necessary efforts to compete and win.

When the academy's superintendent, Lt. Gen. Ken Tallman, offered me the head coaching job on March 3, 1979, little did I know that his tenacious spirit would surround me and the Falcons. Lt. Gen. Tallman decided that Air Force was to be the first service academy to join a college conference. Air Force joined the Western Athletic Conference in 1980. It was a brilliant move.

AFA athletic director Col. John Clune was a warrior for the program and vigorously fought for the athletes in order to be competitive. Air Force football owes all of its success from 1978 to the present to Lt. Gen. Tallman and to Col. Clune.

Our first game in 1979 was against a speedy Tulsa team at Falcon Stadium. Late in the game, a Tulsa back broke loose and outran our whole defense to give the Golden Hurricane the win. Walking off the field to our locker room, I remembered what legendary coach Paul "Bear" Bryant of Alabama had advised: "Always be prepared for your locker-room talk. Be ready to handle a big victory or a close win. Prepare for a huge defeat or a gut-wrenching loss." I had not done this, because all my actions were toward a victory. I never considered that we would lose.

In the locker room, I told our team what Coach Bryant had said, but added that I had not done this. I told them we would grade the game film and that I hoped they were playing as hard on the last play of the game as they were on the first play. The coaching staff graded the film, and I'm proud to say all the players graded 100 percent effort on that last play. Needless to say, this was a good beginning for us.

After the 1979 season, which we finished 2-9, I decided to install the triple-option wishbone offense. I believed this would give us the best chance for success. I had read that successful people do one of two things. One, they do things better than anyone else. Or two, they do things differently. The wishbone formation allowed us to do something different and, if we could execute it, something better.

Fisher DeBerry and I had talked about the wishbone while attending a Fellowship of Christian Athletes conference. Fisher and Jim Brakefield, the head coach at Appalachian State, where Fisher was coaching as an assistant, came and shared their expertise about the wishbone with all of our coaches at the academy. Only a few weeks later, we had an opening on our staff. Fisher and his wife, Lu Ann, graciously accepted the challenge of training Air Force leaders through football.

Late in the third of my five seasons as Air Force's head coach, in November 1981, we found ourselves at Olympic Stadium in Tokyo playing San Diego State at the Mirage Bowl. San Diego State was 6-4, planning on beating a 3-7 Air Force team and going to a postseason bowl game. The first half was a disaster for us, with the Aztecs so dominant, they ran 69 plays on offense. We were delighted to be behind only 16-0 after two quarters of play. Halftime for that game lasted one hour, 10 minutes, much longer than usual because the wonderful Japanese fans wanted to see the bands from both schools and our famous performing falcon.

We managed to regroup, and the second half was all ours. We won 21-16, setting the stage for 8-5 and 10-2 seasons the next two years. That victory over San Diego State established the confidence our players needed to believe that anything was possible. Armed with a victorious attitude, we returned in 1982 and won Air Force's first Commander-in-Chief's Trophy by beating Navy and Army. We also beat Notre Dame (30-17) for the first time in school history and closed the season with the first postseason bowl victory in school history (36-28 over Vanderbilt in the Hall of Fame Bowl). It was a remarkable success story that led to even better years for the Falcons.

Faith in God was the foundation of our program, as well as family time. We decided as a coaching staff to come in early and prepare for football but to go home after practice to be with our families. I am so glad we did.

Chapter Fifteen

JIM BOWMAN

Junior-varsity coach (1958-63, 1975)
Freshman team coach (1964-74)
Associate athletic director for recruiting support (1975-2007)
Hometown: Charlevoix, Mich.
Resides now: Corvallis, Ore.

YOU WON'T FIND ANYONE MORE IMPORTANT OR MORE LOVED THAN JIM IN THE HISTORY OF AIR FORCE ATHLETICS. HE WAS A GREAT FOOTBALL COACH, THEN A GREAT ADMINISTRATOR WHO DEVOTED MOST OF HIS LIFE TO HELPING THE FALCONS SHINE IN ALL SPORTS. JIM RECENTLY WAS INDUCTED INTO THE AIR FORCE ACADEMY ATHLETIC HALL OF FAME, A TERRIFIC HONOR FOR A TERRIFIC MAN. JIM COULD HAVE BEEN A GREAT COLLEGE HEAD COACH HAD HE CHOSEN NOT TO GO INTO ADMINISTRATION. A LOT OF PEOPLE DON'T KNOW THAT HE WAS A SUPER SCOUT AND WAS THE MAN BEHIND THE SCENES OF MANY BIG VICTORIES FOR THE FALCONS. HE HAD A GREAT KNACK FOR PROVIDING THE VERY BEST INFORMATION ON OUR OPPONENTS. EVERY HEAD COACH

NEEDS SOMEONE HE CAN BOUNCE THINGS OFF OF. JIM WAS MY MENTOR IN
ADDITION TO BEING A GREAT NEIGHBOR AND FRIEND.

———

Early in life, my parents instilled in me the concept of always being honest and
truthful in word and deed. They also taught me to respect teachers, coaches and
friends. A lesson I learned from high school sports was to remember who you
are and whom you represent, because your actions and words reflect who you are
throughout your lifetime.

My undergraduate years were spent at the University of Michigan, where I
played football and joined the Air Force ROTC. After graduating from Michigan
in 1956 with a bachelor's degree, I went to Reese Air Force Base in Texas to enter
pilot training. The officers instructing our class were fine role models — selfless
and driven by a strong work ethic — and they easily motivated others through their
example. In return for their commitment to our growth as officers, they expected
us to always give our best.

After arriving at the Air Force Academy, I had an opportunity to work with
five head football coaches: Ben Martin, Bill Parcells, Ken Hatfield, Fisher DeBerry
and Troy Calhoun. Each man quickly became a positive role model, mentor
and friend. Each coach's values and expectations were established as a means to
success. Self-discipline, leadership and work ethic were reflected in the people who
assisted these men in their coaching responsibilities.

In 2006, I was ill with influenza and unable to travel to West Point for
the Falcons' football game against Army for the Commander-in-Chief's Trophy.
Coach DeBerry called me from his hotel before boarding the team bus for the
stadium. He wanted to know how I was feeling and to say he missed my presence
on the trip. With all his responsibilities before such a big game, Coach DeBerry
called out of friendship and concern. Fisher never misses calling friends on
birthdays and special occasions. His thoughtfulness and valuing of relationships is
a core leadership characteristic.

Another facet of Fisher's leadership ability is his great sense of humor.
Fisher's "DeBerryisms" are famous. A couple of my favorites are "99 times out of
10," and "You're walking on thin water." Communication is the foundation of
effective leadership, and humor gives Fisher a unique way of communicating his
message to others.

Throughout my tenure at the Air Force Academy, I was in close contact
with cadets, coaches, faculty, officers and staff. Many of these people have been an

inspiration in my life. The common trait I admire and respect in them is integrity; because I could rely on their integrity, I had faith in their decision making.

The Air Force Academy's core values are "integrity first, service before self and excellence in all we do." The cadets' honor code states: "We will not lie, steal or cheat, nor tolerate among us anyone who does." Following these values builds leadership, honor, loyalty, sportsmanship, selflessness and a strong work ethic. These characteristics are especially important in the face of overwhelming odds on the athletic field or battlefield. Integrity makes you aware of your actions and their consequences.

During the 2001 season, Air Force played Hawaii in Honolulu in a night football game. After the game, the team had free time. Some players broke curfew. The next morning, Coach DeBerry and his assistants had a team meeting where they asked the players who had broken curfew to stay in the room and all other players to leave. Twelve players remained and were suspended from the next game: Six players were seniors and six were starters. Fisher's actions made the Air Force Academy's core values and honor code a reality for these cadets.

Working 49 years in the Air Force Academy athletic department left me with many great memories and beliefs. Winning is a short-lived goal, but the preparation to succeed, in whatever you do, is most important. The quality of your preparation is reflected in the people who surround you. Integrity, honesty, selflessness and commitment help you establish realistic goals and become the best person you can be. Whether the outcome is a win or a loss, never lose faith in yourself.

CHAPTER SIXTEEN

SCOTT BECKER

Fullback
Three-year letterman (1998–2000)
Graduated in 2001
Hometown: Granger, Ind.
Resides now: Napa Valley, Calif.

ONE OF MY GREATEST THRILLS IN COACHING WAS SEEING SCOTT SCORE A TOUCHDOWN AGAINST NOTRE DAME. HE GREW UP IN THE SHADOWS OF NOTRE DAME STADIUM. SCOTT WAS A PUNISHING RUNNER AND ONE OF THE MOST UNSELFISH PLAYERS WE EVER HAD. ALL HE WANTED WAS WHAT WAS BEST FOR THE TEAM. SCOTT AND NATE BEARD WERE A GREAT DUO. SCOTT BROUGHT FAME TO OUR PROGRAM AFTER HIS SENIOR SEASON WHEN HE RECEIVED PRESTIGIOUS POSTGRADUATE SCHOLARSHIPS FROM THE NCAA AND THE NATIONAL FOOTBALL FOUNDATION.

Gen. Douglas MacArthur once said, "On the fields of friendly strife are sown the seeds that on other days and other fields will bear the fruits of victory." I read that quote every day for four years on a sign above the doorway to the Air Force

Academy football practice fields. Those words rang true for me just months after my graduation when I first deployed to foreign fields in the aftermath of the 9/11 terrorist attacks on our country. As a young officer leading troops under dynamic, austere conditions, I relied greatly upon what I had learned while playing football for Air Force and Coach Fisher DeBerry.

Football taught me more about life and leadership than any other experience. Honor, discipline, commitment, teamwork, sacrifice and integrity — these principles are the essence of Air Force football. They are not just buzzwords to display on a poster or write home about. When I played for the Falcons, my teammates and I lived these values day in and day out on the practice fields, in the weight room, in the locker room and, most important, on game day. As an Air Force football player, game day meant facing the opponent on the gridiron during crisp Saturday afternoons in the fall. As an Air Force officer, game day was every day, and it took place in Baghdad and Kandahar. Yet those same principles carried me through.

Long before I ever set foot on Gen. MacArthur's other fields, I was a wide-eyed, 190-pound freshman cadet from the cornfields of Indiana. No one in my family had ever been in the military. My grandfather was a dairy farmer, and his only view on the government was that it stole people's money in the form of taxes. It was quite an adjustment for my mother to lose her son to the military.

As I stepped off the bus for basic cadet training at the base of the Rampart Range, I would discover just how much of an adjustment cadet training would be for *me*. For the next six weeks, I had to perform all kinds of silly but grueling exercises. At least it seemed silly to me at the time. Why couldn't I talk when I wanted to? Who was this guy yelling in my face? Why could I take only five chews before swallowing my food?

Through this training period, I was not a part of the football team. However, the freshman players who were going through the same basic training managed to find each other. My first friend at the Air Force Academy was a football player, Bert Giovannetti. When we finally had a chance to get together as a team, I remember working out in the gym with Bert. We agreed that day that football was the only thing that would make the academy experience bearable.

I spent the fall season of my freshman year on the Falcons' scout team, which meant I was supposed to help emulate the opponent's offense for our varsity defense. In other words, I was a sitting duck for linebackers like Chris Gizzi, who was a senior at the time and a terrific player, one of the best in Air

Force history. Despite getting knocked around every day, my only complaint was when the scout team had to repeat a play. The only reason to repeat a play was because the scout team executed well — too well — against the first-team defense. Taking a hit from guys like Chris was more than enough when he didn't know which play was coming. But now he knew exactly what would be coming. Needless to say, that play would end poorly for the scout team.

While I certainly didn't appreciate it at the time, those hits toughened me up and prepared me for the years ahead. My freshman season was 1997, which the Falcons completed by playing in the Las Vegas Bowl against Oregon and finishing 10-3. As a freshman player on the scout team, I didn't travel with the varsity. But that was a huge motivator for me. I wanted to contribute somehow.

Coach DeBerry gave me that opportunity during the offseason, before my sophomore season of 1998. He called me into his office — my first such one-on-one encounter with the head coach — and asked what I thought about playing fullback. I replied that I would play any position just to get on the field. He then challenged me to put some weight on and get ready for spring football. I'll never forget that first encounter because it was my first indication that Coach DeBerry believed in me.

He had this special way of speaking to his players that was part grandfather, part coach. His folksy, Southern drawl would be accentuated only when he really wanted to emphasize something to you. "Now Scotty, you know them linebackers are gonna come after ya. We need you to put some weight on, son." I went on over the next three seasons to play fullback at 230 pounds. Yet over the next three years, much more would change in me than just my weight.

Five meals a day with a couple of protein shakes will certainly help put weight on, but most of my gains came from a relentless effort in the gym. I had a weight-lifting partner, Nate Beard, a Colorado kid from Grand Junction who pushed me not only in the gym but on the practice fields as well. He also played fullback, so we competed with each other. But that healthy competition nurtured one of my most rewarding friendships. Nate, like so many of the men I was honored to play Air Force football with, is like a brother to me.

I couldn't wait for the 1998 season, my sophomore year, to start because I finally had a chance to contribute to the Falcons at the varsity level. I was so excited to play at Falcon Stadium that I jumped offside during my very first play from scrimmage. A rather ominous beginning, I thought. After that series, I jogged over to our sideline expecting to hear a mouthful from Coach DeBerry.

Instead, he smiled at me and said, "Welcome to the big leagues, son." He always had just the right words to motivate his players. But, of course, he had other ways to motivate you as well. I found myself running up and down a steep hill after practice the following Monday for my rookie penalty.

Air Force's 1998 season turned out to be a year of remarkable success. I played enough as a backup to rush for 144 yards and average 3.6 yards per carry. I got a big taste of what it takes to play big-time college football. We defeated Brigham Young 20-13 in Las Vegas in the Western Athletic Conference championship game, and then finished 12-1 by blowing out Washington 45-25 in the Oahu Bowl in Honolulu. Our only loss that year came in a 35-34 shoot-out with Texas Christian in Fort Worth.

Expectations for the 1999 Falcons were sky-high, and I sensed a change in the way Coach DeBerry handled me. Instead of focusing my attention on my performance, he started expecting me as a junior to focus on the performance of those around me. He was masterful at grooming his players to be leaders. Part of his magic touch, though, came from the recognition that for any team to be successful, it must be led by the players. Coach DeBerry couldn't be in the huddle with us on fourth down and goal. But he didn't need to be. He created a football program that was built on leadership. It was up to the players to develop the kind of team they wanted. As I entered my junior season, I started to feel the responsibility of leadership.

Perhaps it was that responsibility that made the 1999 season sting so badly. We finished only 6-5. The players who would return for the 2000 season as seniors vowed to do whatever it took to get the Falcons back to greatness. During the offseason before my senior year, I worked harder than I ever had. All my senior brothers did the same. We knew that we had to set an example. Nate Beard and I had been weight-lifting partners going on three years at that point. We knew each other's strengths and weaknesses, and we worked to make each other better. By then, we had realized, the fullback position in an option offense was so brutal, it would require at least two players rotating in and out to make it through a full game.

Nate was studying for the same degree in civil engineering that I was working toward. Between classes and football, we probably spent 10 to 12 hours a day together. With so much shared time between us, we began finishing each other's sentences. The bond I shared with Nate is just one example of the brotherhood that we all shared — and continue to do so today with Ryan

Fleming, Corey Nelson, Mike Gallagher, Scotty McKay and more. We were all brothers and remain so because of that unbreakable, strong-as-steel Air Force bond among teammates.

While every game was important, there was one game in particular that had been highlighted on my calendar for four years: Notre Dame. I attended high school near South Bend, Ind., so Notre Dame Stadium was practically my backyard. I finally would have the opportunity to play near the Golden Dome in 2000, my senior season.

It was a big game for me personally, but also for the whole team. We were 5-2 and in contention for a bowl bid, and a victory over the famed Fighting Irish at Notre Dame Stadium would make us very attractive during the bowl selection process. I remember the day of that late October game; I walked out on the field for the first time during warm-ups, and I stared up at Touchdown Jesus. I knew I was on hallowed ground. The game turned out to be a tough fight, one that we would lose 34-31 in overtime in heartbreaking fashion. I didn't play very well and felt deeply that I had let my team down. I was the last one left in the locker room after the game when Coach DeBerry walked up behind me and put his hand on my shoulder. His voice was low but firm. "It's what you do now that counts," he told me. Looking back now, I point to that moment as my transition from boy to man. I learned right then and there what it truly took to deal with despair and pick yourself back up from disappointment. My brothers, my teammates, were counting on me.

I'm proud to say that we didn't lose again that season. Just one week after our crushing loss at Notre Dame, we went to Army and won there 41-27 to complete a Commander-in-Chief's Trophy sweep of our biggest rivals, Navy and Army. We followed the Army game by winning Mountain West Conference games against Colorado State (44-40) and San Diego State (45-24) at Falcon Stadium. We finished the season 9-3 by beating David Carr and Fresno State 37-34 in the Silicon Valley Bowl at San Jose State's stadium.

I remember my last play at Falcon Stadium just as well as I remember my first. Playing against San Diego State, behind the blocking of the offensive linemen that was superb all my three years with the varsity, I plowed into the end zone for my final touchdown. Quite a contrast, remember, to my first play just two years before as a sophomore. Perhaps the change was symbolic of something inside of me — something inside all the Falcons who played for Coach DeBerry. We came from all over the United States, players who weren't supposed to be as good as players at other Division I-A schools. Coach DeBerry started with individuals and finished with a family — Fisher's family. We ate together, studied together, played together and partied together. Most important, we won and lost together.

Coach DeBerry knew he was serving a higher purpose than just winning football games. He knew that his players would someday find themselves on Gen. MacArthur's "other fields." It never was enough for all 11 players on the field to execute the play correctly. All 11 of us had to do it correctly, *together*. To some, that difference may seem slight and insignificant. But the bond — we proudly called it the brotherhood — that formed because of that difference is what enabled us to win football games and succeed in life long after playing for the Falcons.

I've always believed that the true success of a leader is defined not just by wins and losses but by the impact a person has on those around him. By that standard, Fisher DeBerry will go down as one of the finest leaders in college football history. His players are scattered all over the globe now, fighting different kinds of battles. But the family remains strong. The values he instilled in us remain very much alive. Coach DeBerry lives in each of us, Southern drawl and all.

All these years later, I don't remember all of the scores or statistics. But the bonds I built with my brothers are still strong; it's almost unspoken. We are each busy doing something different. Many have families of their own. Life appears far removed from the days of the gridiron. But there is this profound spirit in each of us. We share a sense of commitment to and passion for one another. For four years we shed blood, sweat and tears together. What do we have to show for it? Yes, we have scars and newspaper clippings. But none of that matters. We have each other. And we have a responsibility to live our lives in a way that honors the ideals and values of Air Force Academy football and our coach.

Chapter Seventeen

TROY CALHOUN

———

Quarterback
Four-year letterman (1985–88)
Graduated in 1989
Junior-varsity assistant coach (1993)
Junior-varsity offensive coordinator (1994)
Varsity head coach (2007–present)
Hometown: Roseburg, Ore.
Resides now: Colorado Springs, Colo.

———

TROY WAS ONE OF THE SMARTEST FOOTBALL PLAYERS I WAS EVER AROUND. HE WAS MORE PREPARED FOR THE GAME THAN ANYONE I CAN REMEMBER. HAVING PLAYED FOR THE FALCONS AND GRADUATED FROM THE ACADEMY, NOBODY IS BETTER SUITED OR PREPARED THAN TROY TO BE THE HEAD COACH OF THE FALCONS. HE BROUGHT EXTENSIVE MAJOR COLLEGE AND NFL COACHING EXPERIENCE WITH HIM WHEN HE RETURNED TO AIR FORCE, AND THE FALCONS' SUCCESS WITH HIM IN CHARGE DOESN'T SURPRISE ME AT ALL. THE FIRST TWO TEAMS OF HIS HEAD COACHING CAREER WENT 9-4 AND 8-5 AND PLAYED IN

BOWL GAMES, AND HE WAS THE MOUNTAIN WEST CONFERENCE COACH
OF THE YEAR IN HIS FIRST SEASON BACK. A GREAT START, INDEED.
TROY REALLY WANTS TO WIN, BUT HE HAS FULL SIGHT OF THE PURPOSE
OF FOOTBALL AT THE ACADEMY AND KNOWS THAT IT'S ALL ABOUT
THE PLAYERS AND THEIR DEVELOPMENT. TROY'S PERSONAL QUALITIES
AND INFLUENCE MAKE HIM ONE OF THE BRIGHTEST AND BEST YOUNG
COACHES IN COLLEGE FOOTBALL TODAY.

———

Coach Fisher DeBerry has made a remarkable impact on countless people.
Staggering as the number may be, it is the depth of the relationship with him that
leaves the individuals he touched forever changed.

I first had the opportunity to hear Coach DeBerry's wisdom in early
July 1985, a few days after my arrival at the Air Force Academy for basic cadet
training. I vividly recall our class's first gathering at Arnold Hall on the academy
campus. As many as 80 freshmen were eager to play for the Fighting Falcons.
As the newcomers settled into the ground level of the northeast corner of
the Arnold Hall ballroom, we were welcomed by a voice with a unique blend
of enthusiasm and sincerity that stemmed from a man of enormous spirit.
Following the introduction of each assistant and graduate assistant coach,
Coach DeBerry proceeded to let us know why we were so fortunate to be
attending the Air Force Academy.

Here was a group of 18- and 19-year-olds, many of whom were away from
the comforts of home and family for the first time. Heads were shaved and
all personal belongings stripped. As basic cadets, we would be ground into a
completely different culture. Yet Coach DeBerry asserted that all the challenges
would ultimately serve a tremendous purpose. In this environment, we would
learn the basic elements of character: honesty, unselfishness, passion and
discipline. These traits would prepare us for a future steeped in leadership and
service in the Air Force and all future endeavors.

In the middle of basic cadet training at the Air Force Academy, there is
a traditional Sunday afternoon called "Doolie Dining Out." Each basic cadet
spends approximately five hours at the home of someone closely tied to the
academy. I spent Doolie Dining Out at the DeBerry home. It didn't take long
to sense it was a special and blessed place. As Coach DeBerry flipped burgers on
the grill, he let us know that we would eat "until your belly ouches you." As each
player hung up the phone following the 15 minutes we were allowed to call our

families, we could feel a special camaraderie that would help us get through all of our challenging times at the Air Force Academy.

As a player and assistant for him, it always was evident to me that family was a priority to Coach DeBerry. It's a very basic tenet of leadership and influence that reinforces to young people that there is nothing complicated about being able to respect and love others. Fisher knows he has a wonderful co-pilot in his wife, Lu Ann, and loves to share with others that she will always be the head coach in their house. I remember a January day as a cadet going to the academy's field house to work out and seeing Coach DeBerry pitching batting practice in one of the hitting cages to his teenage son, Joe. Joe went on to become an exceptional baseball player at Clemson, helping lead the Tigers to the College World Series before going on to play professional baseball.

Anyone visiting Coach DeBerry and Mrs. DeBerry at the beach in South Carolina each summer will find them with their daughter Michelle and her children. Coach DeBerry beams as he tells stories about his grandkids. You can tell how proud he is of Michelle for her enormous sense of determination and responsibility in raising and educating her children.

If I had to choose the one principle Coach DeBerry unequivocally stands for, it would be commitment. Commitment to his family, friends, community, church, players, coaches and country; the man gives every bit of his heart to all. Even time zones away, you always know you can call or write to Coach DeBerry. Football's greatest prize is the treasured bond that players and coaches have with one another, and with Coach DeBerry, you forever have a great mentor and friend. Every time you're around him and listen to him, you pinch yourself over how fortunate you are to know him. He is as real and thoughtful as they come. There have been times professionally when I've asked for his guidance or awareness of a place to work or a particular situation. He has always been willing to listen and offer his counsel, and each time I have followed his direction and relied upon his support. There was a time in June 1999 when I brought my future wife, Amanda, by the DeBerrys' South Carolina beach home, and I certainly followed Coach DeBerry's nod of approval on her as well.

The Air Force Academy is the world's finest educational and leadership institution. That distinction requires immense resources, such as remarkable academic facilities, dormitories and athletic fields. However, the academy's greatest strength lies within the caliber of leaders who impact the cadets, who then go on to serve as officers in the Air Force for our country. Fisher DeBerry epitomizes the way the academy develops and builds leaders of character. Coach left an everlasting impact on the Air Force Academy, and our nation should be forever grateful for the enduring lessons and spirit he passed on to so many former cadets, players and coaches.

Chapter Eighteen

LT. COL. RODNEY LEWIS

———

Fullback
Four-year letterman (1987–90)
Graduated in 1991
Hometown: Oklahoma City
Resides now: Alexandria, Va.

———

RODNEY IS ANOTHER GREAT PLAYER IN AIR FORCE HISTORY WHO DID IT THE HARD WAY — THROUGH GOOD OLD-FASHIONED HARD WORK. RODNEY WOULD CUT YOU UP AS A TOUGH INSIDE RUNNER. AS A JUNIOR FULLBACK IN 1989, HE RUSHED FOR 128 YARDS AGAINST SAN DIEGO STATE (AVERAGING 8.5 YARDS PER RUSH), 141 YARDS AGAINST TEXAS-EL PASO (7.4) AND 176 YARDS AGAINST UTAH (7.6). MOST IMPORTANT, RODNEY IS ONE OF THE FINEST GENTLEMEN I HAVE EVER KNOWN. I AM SO PROUD TO SEE HIM HAVING SUCH A GREAT ACTIVE-DUTY AIR FORCE CAREER. HE TRULY IS GENERAL OFFICER MATERIAL.

———

As a child growing up in Oklahoma City, I began playing football at age 5. Then I played each year until I graduated from high school, which culminated in our team playing in the Oklahoma state-championship game. Throughout those early years of my life, I honed my football skills and knew I would have an opportunity to play the great game I loved at the collegiate level. However, I longed for something more than being a member of a winning college football program. I also wanted an engineering degree from a great institution.

During the 1985 football season, I witnessed Coach DeBerry and his Air Force Falcons defeat the University of Texas 24-16 in the Bluebonnet Bowl in Houston. As a kid from Oklahoma, I knew that wasn't an easy task for any football team. After all, Coach Barry Switzer and his Oklahoma Sooners, the 1985 national champions, had barely defeated the Texas Longhorns that season, winning only 14-7 in Dallas. From that point on, I followed Air Force football like a hawk — er, I mean a falcon.

After the 1985 season, Coach DeBerry and his staff offered me an opportunity to visit the campus to get a better understanding of the Air Force Academy's true mission. That mission is developing young people to be the best they can be in every facet of their lives in order to serve our country as Air Force officers. Football is just one of the many tools the Air Force Academy uses to harness a young person's talent, and to my delight, the academy was ranked as one of the top five engineering schools in the country.

Coach Charlie Weatherbie, a former Oklahoma State quarterback who would be my position coach at Air Force, introduced me to Coach DeBerry during my recruiting visit to the academy. I knew instantly that Coach DeBerry was a man of tremendous faith, values and courage. I also knew I wanted to be a part of his team because he would help develop me into the man I wanted to become. Coach DeBerry made no promises about playing time or success. What he did promise was that if I chose to attend the Air Force Academy, I would be challenged like never before, and that if I passed my many military, academic and character-development tests, then I would be challenged further on the football fields of friendly strife. I was sold entirely, and on that day was born a lifelong relationship with the great man. Throughout my years at the academy, Coach DeBerry mentored me and challenged me on and off the football field to become what he always knew I could be.

"Remember who you are!" Those are words Coach DeBerry drilled into us. With those four words, he appealed to us to not only remember who we were each day and what we represented, but what we would be tomorrow. He fully understood that we would grow up to be generals, doctors, attorneys, engineers, pilots and other professionals, serving our nation, families and friends, not NFL players. I have no doubt that several of my teammates will rise to be Air Force general officers someday.

I have several fond mentoring memories of Coach DeBerry. As a freshman, I was fortunate to make the Falcons' varsity traveling squad. My hardest challenge during that school year came not on the football field but in the cadet wing. For an Air Force Academy freshman, my life was extremely busy as I met the demands of military training, academics and football practice. Even with 24 hours in a day, I felt like I needed at least 30 hours to accomplish everything that was being asked of me.

I remember the encouragement Coach DeBerry gave me at one of my lowest points during that difficult school year. "You are special, and you're here for a reason," he said to me. They may seem like small words of encouragement, but they resonated at the right time and place in my life. That was Coach DeBerry. Not only did he know *what* to say, but equally as important, he knew *when* to say those words. He was right, too. With the support of my teammates, including Michael Gant, who was a senior in my freshman squadron, I made it. I even had the opportunity to play in several varsity games as a freshman.

Looking back, I can see that my freshman year laid the foundation of my Air Force Academy experience. And looking back further, I know it was Coach DeBerry who paved the way for me because he challenged me to reach my fullest potential on and off the field.

Fisher DeBerry was our football coach, but he was much more than that. He also was our life-lessons coach. On football trips he would always take the opportunity to explain the importance of historical events. For example, whenever we played the University of Hawaii team in Honolulu, we toured Pearl Harbor and the USS Arizona Memorial. He wanted us to learn vicariously from the sacrifices of others and to understand that we also could be asked to enter into harm's way for our country. Gen. Douglas MacArthur once said, "On the fields of friendly strife are sown the seeds that on other days and other fields will bear the fruits of victory." Coach DeBerry knew that he, too, was sowing seeds for our great nation with the young men he was entrusted to teach.

During my football career at Air Force, our teams enjoyed plenty of success. We played in three bowl games and piled up 29 victories over a four-year period, including 9-4 and 8-4-1 seasons. My senior year was the culmination of all the football and life lessons Coach DeBerry taught me and my teammates. My junior year, the 1989 season, was the senior year for our great quarterback, Dee Dowis. Dee only weighed about 160 pounds "soaking wet," as Coach DeBerry liked to say, but he was nothing short of phenomenal. His senior year, Dee scored six touchdowns and rushed for 249 yards in the season opener, a 52-36 victory over San Diego State at Falcon Stadium. That was our 8-4-1 team, and Dee finished that season as a Heisman Trophy finalist, a terrific honor for a terrific player. He received 15 first-place votes and ended up sixth in the 1989 Heisman balloting, finishing ahead of such great players as Florida running back Emmitt Smith, Brigham Young quarterback Ty Detmer, Notre Dame flanker Rocket Ismail and Penn State running back Blair Thomas.

My senior year was a rebuilding year for the Falcons because we had to overcome the loss to graduation of so many starters, Dee included, from the 1989 team that started out 6-0. The media didn't give the 1990 team much hope for a successful season, not by Air Force standards anyway. But Coach DeBerry demanded the very best from us. We were still the Fighting Falcons, a team to be reckoned with. No single person, no single player was greater than any of our teammates. We would win or lose together, and that would be the ultimate test for our football team.

Every week as the 1990 season progressed, Coach DeBerry would evaluate our opponent and discuss that team's attributes with us during practice. "Rodney, if you can't run any harder than that, their linebackers are going to eat your lunch," he would say. He was the ultimate motivator because he knew what each of his players needed to be their best. I always tried to meet his expectations because I valued his sage leadership.

At the end of the season, after months of Coach DeBerry molding us, we had won enough games to qualify for the prestigious Liberty Bowl in Memphis, Tenn. We were 6-5, and our high-profile opponent would be Ohio State University, a tradition-rich Big Ten Conference power program loaded with future NFL players. I believe we were 17-point underdogs going into that game, and nobody outside of our team thought we could beat the Buckeyes. But what the outsiders didn't know is that Coach DeBerry had molded us into a family, and there was no way we were going to let our brothers down. Before the first snap at that Liberty Bowl, the final game of my Air Force career, we knew we would be victorious. The final score: Air Force 23, Ohio State 11. What a memorable way to go out.

My initial thoughts were on target when I met Coach DeBerry for the first time. He did prove to be a man of tremendous faith, values and courage. He helped develop me into the man I wanted to become. Upon graduation, I received my human-factors engineering degree. Then I attended undergraduate pilot training and received two master's degrees, one from the University of Southern California and the other from the Air Force Institute of Technology.

Those trips our Air Force teams took to Pearl Harbor also served me well, because I did find myself in harm's way in the service of our country. I have flown combat missions in Bosnia, Afghanistan and Iraq. I also served a ground tour in Iraq, where I was proud to be awarded the Bronze Star. I also served as an Air Force legislative liaison, fostering relationships within the U.S. Senate and House of Representatives, and recently I was selected as a finalist for the White House Fellowship program.

I married my high school sweetheart, and we have two wonderful children. I understand completely that being a good husband and father are my most important jobs, thanks to my Air Force football coach. He remains a true mentor and always will be one of the larger positive influences on my life. Football was a tool to teach us the true lessons of life, and Coach DeBerry was the sculptor who shaped us into men dedicated to the service of our country. Thank you, Coach DeBerry, for sharing your wonderful values with us.

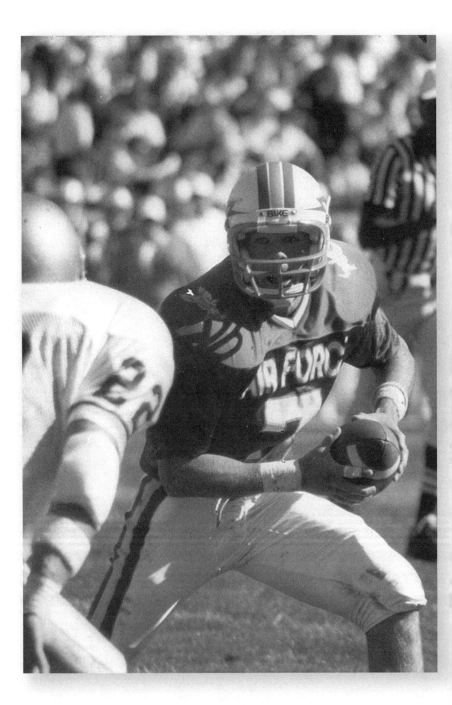

CHAPTER NINETEEN

MAJ. ROB PEREZ

———

Quarterback
Two-year letterman (1990–91)
Graduated in 1992
Hometown: Atlanta
Resides now: Warner Robins, Ga.

———

NEXT TIME YOU HEAR THAT "IT'S ALWAYS TOO SOON TO QUIT," THINK OF ROB. HE WANTED TO STEP OUT OF THE PROGRAM AT THE BEGINNING OF HIS JUNIOR YEAR. I CONVINCED HIM TO HANG IN THERE, AND THE REST IS HISTORY. ROB'S PATIENCE PAID OFF. HE MADE THE MOST OF HIS OPPORTUNITY. HE IS THE ONLY PLAYER IN THE HISTORY OF THE LIBERTY BOWL TO WIN THE MVP AWARD TWO YEARS IN A ROW, LEADING OUR TEAM TO BIG WINS OVER OHIO STATE AND MISSISSIPPI STATE. ROB'S UNDERSTANDING OF OUR OFFENSE AND HIS TOUGHNESS MADE HIM ONE OF THE MOST EFFECTIVE OPTION QUARTERBACKS EVER. ROB WASN'T FLASHY; HE WAS JUST A WINNER AND A DYNAMIC LEADER FOR HIS TEAMMATES.

———

Every time I reflect on my time as an Air Force Academy football player, I see it split into two different eras. During my first two-plus years with the Falcons, I put on my cleats every day and competed against the varsity's first-team defense as the scout team's quarterback. My goal was to play as hard as possible on every play because it would get the defense ready to play that week, and it also might catch the coach's eye. For two years I watched Dee Dowis, the starter, and Lance McDowell, the top backup, running our triple-option offense, and I longed to be in either quarterback's shoes.

I came to the Air Force Academy feeling pretty good about my chance to be the heir apparent to Dee Dowis because I believed I was the only recruit who ran what I called a "true" wishbone offense in high school. So even though I walked out for the first day of practice with 17 other guys at my position, I felt I had a big advantage.

When fall practices began in 1988, my freshman year, I enjoyed some success as the scout team's quarterback. But I never stood out. During one particular practice, my chance of earning a spot on the varsity team as an underclassman took a big hit. Charlie Weatherbie, our quarterbacks coach for the varsity squad and a former quarterback at Oklahoma State, saw Ron Gray scramble out of the pocket on the scout team and run like a deer. Coach Weatherbie stopped to watch and then told Troy Calhoun, our quarterbacks coach for the junior varsity, to "give him the ball again." Ron did it again, but faster and better this time. He became the heir apparent to Dee at the quarterback position.

This was the beginning of my two-year learning curve. I found some relief at the beginning of my sophomore year, in 1989, because Ron was moved to running back on varsity. The third-string quarterback position on the varsity team was open, and I thought my name was a lock for the job, until Charlie Kuhl ran a freakish 4.3-something in the 40-yard dash. I took my "blazing" 4.75-second time in the 40 to the scout team for another year.

The good Lord blesses us in many ways, but our selfish desires often blind us so we can't see them. I played in several junior-varsity games and got a lot of repetitions with the majority of the players who were starters on the varsity team the next season. We won some great games on the junior varsity squad, beating teams like Nebraska's JV squad and Brigham Young's JV squad. My dad still remembers the junior-varsity game when we beat BYU in the final minute. I sometimes think it was more exciting for him to watch me play in that game than in any of the games I played for the Falcons on the varsity team.

When my sophomore season came to an end, I had been lucky enough to dress for two varsity games. I was disappointed I had not experienced more success. Every time I looked at the depth chart, hoping to see my name move up, I was disappointed.

During a Fellowship of Christian Athletes meeting, I was introduced to a Bible passage from the book of James that became my mantra: "Consider it pure joy, my brothers, whenever you face trials of many kinds, because you know that the testing of your faith develops perseverance. Perseverance must finish its work so that you may be mature and complete"(James 1:2-4). I know these trials I describe seem trivial, but as a 21-year-old young man, I dreamed of playing varsity, and nothing else seemed more important to me at the time.

The first era of my Air Force football career continued into my junior year. I was battling for the No. 2 spot on the depth chart behind Ron Gray. I often prayed for an opportunity to play in just one varsity game so I could prove to myself that I could compete at that level. I was very close to quitting football several times, but thankfully I came to the conclusion that being a part of the team in any capacity was better than leaving.

After I got over the frustration of not getting the opportunities I wanted and began appreciating the great opportunity I had as part of the Air Force team, my perspective shifted. I played without a tremendous weight on my shoulders and just had a good time competing. I still fought and scratched every time I walked on the field, but I learned my most valuable life lesson. When I stopped worrying about me and put my efforts into the team, wonderful things started happening. The best of these things was that I was enjoying the ride even though I wasn't playing. And as I soon found out, that part about not playing would change.

Air Force's fourth game of the 1990 season, my junior year, was against Wyoming in Laramie. Ron Gray tweaked his knee in warm-ups. I had been named the top backup, so I was ready to go. On the third play of the game, Ron made a cut and suffered a torn knee ligament. I was excited for the opportunity to play, but I still hate that Ron played only one full varsity season because of knee problems. I got my chance, but I pressed so hard that I made many mistakes. Wyoming beat us 24-12, and I lost the starting job for the next game against San Diego State.

Two weeks after the Wyoming game, the coaching staff called on me to come in for the second half of the Navy game at Falcon Stadium. We were 2-3 at the time and needed a victory to get back on track. We did just that, winning 24-7. I had won the starting job. The following weekend, I lived my dream. I started my first Division I-A game against the University of Notre Dame at the famed Notre Dame Stadium. I am the youngest of seven kids, and my whole family traveled to see the game, as well as many of my high school coaches. What a thrill. Even though we lost 57-27 to the Fighting Irish, we did some good things offensively.

The second era of my Air Force career began at that Notre Dame game. The two teams I was lucky enough to be a part of did some great things. In 1990 we beat Army (15-3) at West Point for the first time in eight years. We won back-to-back Liberty Bowls against Ohio State (23-11) and Mississippi State (38-15), when both opponents were big favorites. Our blowout of Mississippi State was my final game with the Falcons. My senior year, we finished 10-3 and were ranked in the nation's top 25. These remain fantastic memories, but in some ways I cherish my first two years with the Falcons more because I learned so much about myself and about life. Those first two years really defined who I am today.

Everyone who played for Coach DeBerry is blessed to have done so. If I were to send my son off to play football in college, I couldn't think of a better man to teach, coach and mentor him. Fisher DeBerry was a great football coach who truly cared for everyone in the Air Force family. This family philosophy made him an effective coach.

The words he would say every Saturday after a game or practice still stick with me: "Men, three things: First, tomorrow is the Lord's Day. I expect you to go to church and thank Him for all of your blessings. Second, call your parents and tell them you love them and thank them for supporting you so that you could come to the Air Force Academy. They are the reason you are here. Finally, when you go out this weekend, don't forget who you are and who you represent." Those were very powerful words spoken to very impressionable young men. Imagine how strong our society would be today if every young person had someone who cared enough about them to pass that message on to them.

My sincere thanks go especially to Coach DeBerry, to Patty and Chuck Leggiero, to Coach Cal McCombs and Mrs. McCombs, to my brothers and sisters and most of all to my mother and father. Some of the happiest times I remember spending with my parents, brothers and sisters were before and after my games. Nikki, my beautiful wife, says I am like a little kid when I get to go back to the Air

Force Academy and see a game at Falcon Stadium. I have been blessed with three wonderful children — Abner, Polly and Ripp — who love to cheer on the Fighting Falcons in Colorado.

Chapter Twenty

MAJ. ANTHONY ROBERSON (RET.)

———

Halfback
Three-year letterman (1986–88)
Graduated in 1989
Junior varsity assistant head coach (2007–08)
Hometown: Colorado Springs, Colo.
Resides now: Colorado Springs, Colo.

———

IT ONLY TOOK ME TWO YEARS BEFORE I WAS SMART ENOUGH TO KNOW HOW BEST TO USE THIS HUMAN DYNAMO. OUR COACHING STAFF KNEW ANTHONY HAD SPEED AND QUICKNESS, BUT WE WORRIED ABOUT HIS SMALL SIZE. ANTHONY IS A CLASSIC EXAMPLE IN FOOTBALL OF WHY THE SIZE OF YOUR HEART IS MUCH MORE IMPORTANT THAN THE SIZE OF YOUR BODY. ROBY WAS AS TOUGH AS THEY COME AND HAD MANY BIG PLAYS FOR THE FALCONS ONCE WE LOCKED HIM INTO BEING A HALFBACK. AS A JUNIOR IN 1987, HE RUSHED FOR 110 YARDS AND THREE TOUCHDOWNS AGAINST NEW MEXICO ON JUST SEVEN CARRIES. THAT'S A WHOPPING AVERAGE OF 15.7 YARDS PER RUSH! HE WAS THE 1988 WINNER OF OUR PRESTIGIOUS BRIAN BULLARD MEMORIAL AWARD, THE HIGHEST HONOR

ANY AIR FORCE PLAYER CAN RECEIVE. ROBY WAS JUST A JOY TO COACH
BECAUSE OF HIS GREAT ENTHUSIASM AND LOVE FOR THE GAME. MORE
IMPORTANT, HE WENT ON TO BECOME ONE OF AIR FORCE'S BEST AND
MOST COMPETITIVE FIGHTER PILOTS.

I spent most of my 20 years of active-duty service in the Air Force in the cockpit
of an F-16 Falcon, one of the world's great jet fighters. When I left the flight line
to return to the sideline as a member of the Air Force Academy football coaching
staff before my retirement as an Air Force airman, I had more than 2,200 hours
of flight time in the F-16, including 101 combat missions. One mission stood out
above all the others.

It was late summer in 1995, after my proud participation in Operation
Provide Comfort and Operation Deny Flight and before my equally proud
contributions supporting Operation Enduring Freedom and Operation Iraqi
Freedom. After a night strike against military targets in Bosnia during Operation
Deliberate Force, I was flying over the Adriatic Sea back to Aviano Air Base
in Italy, where my group of F-16s from the famed 555th Fighter Squadron was
headquartered. The attack had occurred at 2 o'clock in the morning, and we had
hit an ammunition storage depot. I had just dropped two 2,000-pound, laser-
guided bombs and had destroyed my precision target. As I flew back to Aviano
over the moonlit Adriatic, I reflected on the mission, on everything that had led
me to that extraordinarily serious point of my life. And I thought of one man:
Fisher DeBerry.

I read that the typical coach throughout a career influences about 25,000
people. Well, Coach DeBerry is far above that number. He's the ace of aces when
it comes to coaches. If we could put a finger on all the people he influenced as a
coach, as a man and as a leader, we could probably start our own nation. That's
why I thought of him the night of that mission. I told myself that I had to call
him, just to hear his voice, as soon as possible after I returned to base. I knew
his soothing, reassuring voice would bring much-needed calm to my life at that
particular point. Operation Deliberate Force was part of the Bosnian conflict and
was planned to bring a vicious bully, Slobodan Milosevic, to the bargaining table
and end the atrocities in his country.

The first night of that conflict, I had the great responsibility of leading
men and women of coalition forces from several nations into combat. As I sat in
the briefing room planning for that mission, a 2 a.m. strike on the No. 1 target

on our target list, I thought back to my special time at the Air Force Academy when guys just like me were on the football field in a huddle at a decisive moment during a game, and collectively we had to make the most of our skills and achieve an important mission. Well, we all had a very successful mission that night. We all hit our targets, and we all came back alive. And the end of the campaign was a success.

But what I felt that night is what made that mission my most memorable. I had to think about the greater good, no question. We were in combat operations to stop atrocities against innocent people. That's why, on a July day in 1985, I raised my right hand on the grounds of the Air Force Academy and committed myself to a cause that was greater than I was and greater than the entire Air Force. But once you're in combat operations, you naturally think about a lot of things that come with your involvement, before, during and after combat, because you have to live with the result. Now, the 21-year-old U.S. Marine on a street corner he sees it and hears it and feels it day in and day out. It's usually much more personal to him. For an Air Force airman, executing the type of mission I was executing that night from 25,000 feet, it's different, because you see other people become part of the precision target.

During the time of releasing and guiding my weapons, I witnessed some military men drive up to that ammunition storage depot we were about to destroy. They were at the target when it was hit. So there's no doubt in my mind those men lost their lives during that strike. Yes, they were classified as the enemy because we were engaged in combat. But we're still talking about human lives. I was more in touch with the reality of my duty after that mission than I ever was before. As a fighter pilot, I certainly understood the consequences of combat. It's just that on that particular strike mission, I witnessed it myself and truly felt responsible.

That's why I called Coach DeBerry. Coach helped me understand that on that very important mission, with reality literally at my fingertips, I was able to make the right decision and execute the game plan, living with the result and being able to defend it and explain it someday to my own children.

Nothing about me is solely me. I'm thankful to say that I was guided and moved in the direction my life took. If you were to write the ending of my story based on what you knew about me the first 13 or 14 years of my life, it probably would be "incarcerated" or "murdered." I'm not kidding. I was born in Sacramento, Calif., and I grew up in a really rough part of Oakland. I was raised by my maternal grandmother, Billie Brooks. My parents divorced when I was very young. My mother was challenged, economically and educationally. And she became a substance abuser.

My grandmother Billie was an entertainer on the East Coast at the time. My siblings and I became the property of the state and were briefly entered into a foster-care circuit. So my grandmother left her entertainment lifestyle — she was a beautiful and wonderful singer — to come to Oakland and raise me and my siblings, until she became terminally ill with cancer. She devoted the time she had remaining to reintroduce me to my father and convince him to bring me back to him. After she died, I went to live with my father, James Roberson, a wonderful man and career Army man who was stationed at Fort Carson near Colorado Springs. Today, he not only is my father and a beloved grandfather to my five children; he is one of my best friends. I love him dearly.

My grandmother will always be my source of inspiration. She's forever my angel. She didn't share with us how sick she really was until it was almost over. My surroundings in Oakland were bleak, but she always made it seem better. I lived in a low-income neighborhood with a lot of violence and a lot of drugs. Growing up at 5451 Princeton Street in Oakland, I didn't have a lot of external reasons for hope. But I had the best grandmother, the best person in the whole world, on my side. She always had a vision for me that was greater than the circumstances around me. Interestingly enough, there weren't many athletics in her vision. It was always school and school and more school. She demanded that I be academically sound and solid in my faith. Those were the pillars of success to her.

Grandma Billie taught me to be a man of character. She told me there should never be anyone on the planet who puts forth more effort than I did. She always told me the foundation of any good relationship is trust. And she taught me how to be self-sufficient and independent, which really helped me when I went to live with my father, who didn't have a lot of parenting experience at the time. Believe me when I say that without her, I wouldn't be here talking to you. She liked to say, "There's always going to be people who come into your life, and you will know it when they are the genuinely good ones."

Although Grandma Billie didn't know it, she was preparing me for my experience at the Air Force Academy, where I found my ticket to great opportunity. It was up to me to put forth the effort and earn that ticket, but it definitely was there for the taking. Had I not become a success in life, it wouldn't have been the academy's fault. It would have been my fault. From two consecutive seasons of leading the Western Athletic Conference in all-purpose yardage, to a National Strength and Conditioning Association selection as an All-American athlete, to becoming the only Air Force Falcon in the history of our football program to be honored with our top three major awards (Brian Bullard Memorial Award, Mr. Intensity Award and MVP), to graduating with military distinction in 1989, my opportunities turned into success. This success was a direct result of the power of influence my grandmother Billie and a few others have had on my life.

Since my grandmother Billie's passing, my paternal grandmother, Sylvia Cross — we affectionately call her "Big Momma" — continues to be my beacon of love, sacrifice, commitment and service. Like my grandmother Billie, my Big Momma strongly believes in the same key pillars of a successful life: character, effort, trust, self-sufficiency, independence and faith. Her living example continues to sustain me, and the linkage through her to my grandmother Billie is as powerful as it has ever been. I am forever grateful to my grandmothers, and to the one gentleman who loved me and led me to my saving grace.

Brent Garretson was the first coach in organized sports with whom I came in contact in Colorado Springs. He was a basketball coach at the middle school I was attending, and I was a little bitty point guard on his team of eighth-graders. Brent will do anything to help kids, and I'm proof of that. He's the same way today. He will pour himself out on anyone in need. I can't say enough good things about him.

Without these great influences in my life, my path would have been much different. I am the most blessed, undeserving person on the planet. To have the opportunity to do what I've done, to see what I've seen — I don't deserve those things. What enabled it? Well, the relationships I've developed with people of great character, people who love unconditionally and know the value of hard work, commitment and service. From my grandmother Billie to my Big Momma to Brent to Coach DeBerry, I received the valuable lessons necessary for a successful life.

To Coach DeBerry: Your players are all better people because of your teachings, your coaching, your guidance, your love and your consummate example. Your power to influence continues to pay forward, making all of us better leaders for our nation and better disciples and witnesses for our God. I love you, Coach DeBerry, and I owe you the world. *Win!*

I had no idea what I wanted to do with my Air Force career when I enrolled at the academy. I just knew I wanted to live my life focused on service. I also knew I believed in the mission of the academy, in the role of the Air Force in our nation's defense. I saw a few Air Force football games when I was a Sierra High School student. It became a passion to be constantly tuned in to what was going on at Falcon Stadium. I aspired to put that famous Air Force lightning bolt on the side of my football helmet and join this legacy of excellence created by the scores of men who came before me.

When I came back to the Air Force Academy to coach as a member of Troy Calhoun's staff, I went on a recruiting trip where I had the privilege of meeting with a number of impressive young men across the country. I stood before each of them as evidence of what the academy experience could do for them. I told them, "If you believe in who you are, if you want to make a great contribution to our nation, if you want to grow up to be a person of influence, a leader with character, then you come to the Air Force Academy. And by the way, you're going to play on a football team with other young men who believe in the same things you believe in. And you're going to win, on the field and in life."

I am part of an organization of people who eat and sleep and breathe honor and character and integrity. To this day, I can pick up the phone and call any academy graduate, and I know what they stand for, how they're going to respond to adversity, and exactly who they are. Although our nation's three service academies are distinctly different in their missions, they're all developing young men and women of character to be leaders of our country.

My retirement ceremony, the first of its kind, was conducted in Iraq at Balad Air Base. I retired after being honored with the opportunity to return four original Tuskegee Airmen back to their namesake unit, which is currently operational in Iraq: the 332nd Air Expeditionary Wing. During World War II, they were all members of the famed 332nd Fighter Group. These gentlemen honored me at my ceremony at the conclusion of their trip back to the Tuskegee Wing. As you can imagine, the culmination of these events was an emotionally moving experience.

I'm also honored to say that the Air Force airman I hold in the highest regard, Lt. Gen. Gary L. North, retired me. He is a warrior's warrior, an unrivaled leader and a true fighter pilot. At the time of my ceremony, he was the commander in charge of the air operations in Iraq and Afghanistan and commanded the courageous airmen deployed to U.S. Central Command. He also was the 9th Air Force commander and led all the active, guard and reserve wings in the southeastern United States. He recently was nominated for his fourth star and will continue to serve our nation in the highest capacity as a military officer. "Nordo" is my model for excellence in leadership and military service.

My hat goes off to everyone who coordinated the live video teleconference in Colorado Springs that enabled my family to be a part of the ceremony in Iraq. The 10th Communications Squadron and my brothers in the Air Force Academy football office did everything possible to make sure it all went off without a hitch. I owe you greatly for this enduring memory.

When I returned home, Deuce, my oldest son, embraced me and told me that he was very proud of me. He said, "Dad, you should be proud. You fought the good fight, you finished the course and you kept the faith. And that's what you always say to me." He was quoting 2 Timothy 4:7, the verse my three oldest children and I memorized to remind each other to give ourselves in honor of our family and our God. I had never felt such powerful emotion. To be reassured by my son Deuce was the one sign I needed to know that everything I did was not a fruitless effort.

I fought hard for my country, and in the shadow of that commitment, I took great pride in carrying on the tradition of service that was born from a remarkable experiment in the 1940s. And from that experiment – the legendary Tuskegee Experiment – our nation was changed, benefiting us all. To have my 7-year-old son recognize that is a great testament to all of us. We are the window to the future of our nation, and the first glance begins in our homes.

Let us all remember that it is fate to be born free, it is a privilege to live free and it is a responsibility to die free.

Chapter Twenty-One

Jappy Oliver

———

Defensive line coach (1995–2002)
Hometown: Flint, Mich.
Resides now: South Bend, Ind.

———

WHEN JAPPY WAS COACHING AT VANDERBILT, THE COMMODORES'
DEFENSIVE STAFF VISITED THE ACADEMY. I WAS REALLY IMPRESSED
WITH JAPPY'S KNOWLEDGE OF FOOTBALL AND WITH HIS HUMOR. HE REALLY
KNEW THE GAME AND ENJOYED EVERY MINUTE OF COACHING. JAPPY WAS
AN IMMACULATE DRESSER AND A GREAT RECRUITER BECAUSE OF HIS PEOPLE
SKILLS. HE ACCEPTED COACHING OPPORTUNITIES AT SOUTH CAROLINA
UNDER LOU HOLTZ AND MOST RECENTLY AT NOTRE DAME. HE HAD A LOT
TO DO WITH BRYCE FISHER'S REMARKABLE DEVELOPMENT AS AN AIR FORCE
DEFENSIVE LINEMAN, AND BRYCE ENDED UP IN THE NFL.

———

I really don't know whether I chose the coaching profession or whether the
coaching profession chose me. I remember my high school coaches telling me
that based on the way I played football, they thought I would make a good coach

someday. I'm glad they saw that in me, because I can't imagine doing anything else more enjoyable or rewarding.

I was the defensive line coach for the University of Notre Dame football program 2005–08, following two seasons at South Carolina, and I look back at my eight years on Fisher DeBerry's Air Force coaching staff as a tremendous privilege. The core values the Air Force Academy is built upon stayed with me during my time at Notre Dame, as I'm sure they have with all of Fisher's former players across the country. Values such as the academy's all-important honor code: "We will not lie, steal or cheat, nor tolerate among us anyone who does." As well as this: "Integrity first, service before self and excellence in all we do." Believe me, you will be a better person if you let those words guide you in your daily life.

Many of the best years I've had in coaching came as a member of Coach DeBerry's staff. We enjoyed a lot of success at Air Force. I never will forget our 20-17 overtime victory at Notre Dame Stadium in 1996, when the Fighting Irish were ranked No. 8 in the country. But to me, our 1998 season at Air Force stands out most because of how dominant we were on both sides of the ball. That year the Falcons won the Western Athletic Conference championship by beating Brigham Young 20-13 in Las Vegas and finished 12-1.

But most important is the lesson I learned about the power of influence. Several of my players have gone on to have successful careers in the NFL. While I am very happy for them and proud of their accomplishments, what means the most to me are the phone calls I get from my players, from all walks of life, calls thanking me for helping them achieve success in their career fields. You don't have to play in the NFL to consider yourself a success, but you do have to be a good person to honestly feel successful. To think that I have helped shape the lives of so many good young men, well, that's the wonderful reward you find in the coaching profession.

My parents had the most influence on my life just by the way they took care of their business every day. Both of them were exceptionally hard workers and retired from factory jobs. As far as my coaching career is concerned, it was my high school football coach, Dar Christiansen, who eventually offered me my first job in this great profession. Many of the things I learned from Dar are things I still find useful today, and that is worthy of a salute to him.

The care and love Coach DeBerry continues to have for everyone in his "football family" remain a constant reminder of the right way to go about coaching. To this day, my mother always asks me how Coach DeBerry is doing and tells me to thank him for keeping in contact with her through cards and letters. That is pretty powerful.

Air Force was a consistent winner during the Fisher DeBerry era because Coach was so consistent in doing his work and living his life the right way. After every Saturday scrimmage or game, he made sure to remind his players and staff that we didn't get there by ourselves, that we should go to church on Sundays, and that we needed to call home and tell the people most responsible for our success — our parents — that we loved them and appreciated all they did for us.

Thank you, Fisher, for giving me the opportunity to coach with you at the Air Force Academy.

Chapter Twenty-Two

COL. BART WEISS

―――――

Quarterback
Three-year letterman (1983–85)
Graduated in 1986
Hometown: Naples, Fla.
Resides now: Wichita, Kan.

―――――

QUARTERBACKS DON'T COME ANY TOUGHER THAN BART, WHO WAS THE PRIMARY PILOT OF OUR 12-1 TEAM IN 1985 THAT SHARED THE WESTERN ATHLETIC CONFERENCE CHAMPIONSHIP AND DEFEATED TEXAS IN THE BLUEBONNET BOWL. HE HAD A GREAT SENIOR SEASON, RUSHING FOR 1,032 YARDS AND PASSING FOR 1,449 YARDS ON THAT 1985 TEAM, WHICH LED THE NATION IN VICTORIES AND CAME CLOSE TO PLAYING FOR A NATIONAL CHAMPIONSHIP. LIKE MOST OF OUR PLAYERS, BART HAD TO WAIT FOR HIS CHANCE TO PLAY. AND WHEN HE GOT HIS OPPORTUNITY, HE REALLY TOOK ADVANTAGE OF IT. HE LED US TO SOME REALLY BIG WINS OVER SOME GREAT PROGRAMS. AFTER GUIDING US TO A 23-7 VICTORY OVER VIRGINIA TECH IN THE 1984 INDEPENDENCE BOWL, I JOKINGLY WARNED BART NOT TO TAKE A SHOWER IN FRONT OF HIS MOTHER. I DIDN'T

WANT HER TO SEE HOW BEAT UP HE WAS AFTER THAT GAME. SHE PROBABLY WOULD HAVE KILLED ME FOR PUTTING HIM IN SUCH DANGER. BUT BART TOOK OVER THAT GAME AND DOMINATED MAYBE THE BEST DEFENSE WE EVER PLAYED AGAINST WHILE I WAS AT THE ACADEMY, A DEFENSE THAT FEATURED BRUCE SMITH.

———————

"There is a lot of give and take in the world today, but not a lot of people willing to give what it takes."

"The difference between Champ and Chump is U."

"There is no I in the letter team."

"Play your best this play."

"You make the difference."

Each day before football practice, I heard these unique sayings from Coach DeBerry, who was my position coach on Ken Hatfield's staff, and even after he succeeded Coach Hatfield as head coach of the Falcons. These sayings help guide my life and my family. They help in leading our terrific young airmen in the world's most professional and lethal Air Force.

My favorite saying from Coach DeBerry is "You make the difference." Playing, training or working as one team and doing your very best each day, on every mission or sortie definitely makes a difference. Putting that philosophy to work has created wonderful opportunities for me in and out of the Air Force.

I cannot remember a day when I haven't used some lesson learned while I was an Air Force cadet or a football player for the Falcons. A wide range of experiences help to fuel my leadership and ability to overcome adversity. On the icy practice fields late in the fall, my hands would sometimes get so cold, it seemed impossible to grip the ball, throw a pass or think through the myriad defensive fronts we might encounter. In early summer practices, I gutted out repetitive option-play scenarios and ran sprints we called "gassers" after long practices. We played through the heat and exhaustion to make the one play that could have been the difference in Air Force winning or losing.

My junior year was the 1984 season, Coach DeBerry's first season as Air Force's head coach. We were playing Navy, our favorite nemesis, at Falcon Stadium in early October. On one particular play, I played the triple option all the way into the Navy secondary. While racing down the field about 30 or 40 yards, I caught one of our halfbacks, Jody Simmons, out of the corner of my eye.

Remarkably, we were keeping our "pitch relationship" — that's an option-offense term — the entire way, just as we had practiced it a thousand times.

With only two Navy defensive players left to beat, I pitched the ball back to Jody, who went on to score the game-turning touchdown. He was credited with a 47-yard touchdown run and finished the game with 100 yards on just 16 carries. We won 29-22, and that option play Jody scored on epitomizes the great strength of Air Force football. It captures the idealistic integrity of 11 men playing for a common purpose, each performing his assignment flawlessly while unselfishly yielding the glamour of scoring a touchdown to the teammate who was in the best place at the best time.

One week later, we were playing at Notre Dame Stadium. I still can vividly recall our bus ride from the team hotel in Elkhart, Ind., to the Notre Dame campus in South Bend. My father attended Notre Dame, and this was the first time I was able to see Touchdown Jesus and the hallowed ground that Paul Hornung, Joe Montana, Joe Theismann, Knute Rockne and so many others in the Fighting Irish family made famous. I'm guessing Notre Dame had at least 50 players who had been high school All-Americans. I don't think the Falcons had even one.

We were giving up 50 to 60 pounds per player at the line of scrimmage, on both sides of the ball. I remember thinking to myself, "What are we doing here?" I knew how David must have felt about Goliath before they tangled. This can't be done, right? Well, we ended up crushing the Irish. We won 21-7, and the game wasn't that close. We had 24 first downs to Notre Dame's 14. We had 371 yards rushing to Notre Dame's 90. We had 398 total yards to Notre Dame's 207. Our defense was fantastic. Jody rushed for 141 yards on just 24 carries, and I scored our last touchdown on a 5-yard run. It was a euphoric feeling being part of an Air Force victory at Notre Dame Stadium. To this day, I can think of no other experience that better reinforces what true confidence, determination and teamwork can do for anyone who faces what they deem to be insurmountable odds.

Everybody's senior year is special, but mine seemed extraordinarily special, because after we went 8-4 and beat Virginia Tech 23-7 in the Independence Bowl my junior year, we went 12-1 in 1985 and led the nation in victories. I'm biased, but I believe that 1985 team ranks as the best team in the history of Air Force football. We had unmatched pride in, and admiration for, one another. We won our first four games by 42, 42, 42 and 37 points and ended up sharing the Western Athletic Conference title with Brigham Young, the defending national champion. We beat Navy 24-7 at Annapolis and Army 45-7 at Falcon Stadium. We started 10-0 and were ranked as high as No. 4 in the national polls. Yet we didn't dominate everybody we played. We had to replace key players who were sick and missed some games, and we had our share of injuries. We beat Notre Dame 21-15 at Falcon Stadium after trailing late in the game. Terry Maki, our great linebacker, blocked a field goal that we ran back for the winning touchdown. Our only loss, 28-21 at BYU, cost us a chance to play for the national championship. But we regrouped and beat Hawaii 27-20 in Honolulu to clinch a share of the WAC title and then finished an unbelievable season with a 24-16 victory over Texas in the Bluebonnet Bowl. That season was definitely a landmark year for Air Force football. The adversity we overcame defined that team, not the lopsided victories.

For me, football and the Air Force Academy are intertwined. I learned as much about character, leadership, integrity and professional soldiering from our practices and games as I did from my academics and military studies. Coach DeBerry enhanced the mission of the academy by producing leaders of character. I feel I learned more than the average cadet who didn't get that extra time down at the field house, where on a daily basis we were able to apply those academic lessons of leadership and military history.

Coach DeBerry actively taught us about maintaining balance — the kind of balance we needed to juggle a heavy academic load of 17 to 21 credit hours per semester with our military drills and the demands of being an intercollegiate athlete. Coach DeBerry's lessons went far beyond the gridiron and bleachers. Black and white choices are easily discernable, but Coach DeBerry shined light on those gray areas and often drew upon adversity and real-life scenarios to more clearly delineate right from wrong. When faced with difficult challenges in my life today, I often lean on those years of mentoring under Coach DeBerry, and they have become powerful guides to help me determine the best option for the greater good.

As I move from the Pentagon after two years to another Air Force command opportunity — this time to Wichita as the 22nd Operations Group commander at McConnell Air Force Base, where 60 KC-135 Stratotanker refueling aircraft, five squadrons and about 900 people will be my responsibility — I continue to remind myself of my days at the academy. President Harry S.

Truman was fond of saying, "It's amazing what you can accomplish when you don't care who gets the credit." That is the Air Force Academy I remember, the Falcons team I was so proud to represent.

Chapter Twenty-Three

PAUL HAMILTON

Quarterbacks and fullbacks coach (1990-96)
Fullbacks coach (2006)
Hometown: Charleston, S.C.
Resides now: Brevard, N.C.

It was my privilege to coach Paul at Appalachian State. What a competitor he was. Paul grew up in a coaching family, so I knew he would be a great football coach. He has such a great understanding of the game. Paul did wonderful work with our quarterbacks. He has now been a head coach at three colleges. Two of Paul's children were in our daughter's wedding, and our middle granddaughter, Alanna, was named after Paul and Jane's youngest daughter. What a beautiful family Paul has, and what a knowledgeable coach he is. Paul probably did the best coaching job in the country in 2007 at Brevard, where he took the job on July 1. He had to assemble a coaching staff, recruit some players and then train his staff by Aug. 1, when the Brevard players

REPORTED FOR PRACTICE. BREVARD PLAYED ITS FIRST GAME JUST 23 DAYS
LATER AND BARELY LOST TO A NATIONALLY RANKED TEAM.

————

As the head football coach at Brevard College in North Carolina, I look back
with great pride and appreciation for my coaching opportunity at the Air Force
Academy. I cherish the growth I gained spiritually, the joy and bonding those days
brought to my family, and the impact so many people had on my development as
a coach and person. My experience at the Air Force Academy confirmed to me
what caring and commitment to one another means.

I am very thankful for the friendship and support that so many gave
to my family and me during our years at the academy. I pray they all know
how much they mean to me, from Coach DeBerry and Lu Ann DeBerry to
all of the incredible assistant coaches I worked with, such as Chuck Petersen;
the administration, including Jim Bowman; terrific secretaries such as Kathy
Shipley; the strong support staff; spiritual leaders and, without question, the
group of players I was so blessed to have the privilege to coach. All of them were
and have been such a strong influence in my life. Their willingness to give of
themselves and stand strong for the morals and values of what Air Force football
and life are about continues to mean so much to me today. Their support, along
with my family and faith in God, were such a strength to me through times of
adversity at the academy and as I've moved forward in my life.

My Christian faith is very important to me. I hope and pray I demonstrated
this, though I know I fall short every day of the person I need to be. I thank the
Lord for Coach DeBerry, the other coaches I worked with and the spiritual leaders
who were such outstanding Christian role models for me at the academy and
beyond. As I hit life's potholes, I am thankful for the strength my faith in God has
given me. As a head coach, I talk to my players about the source of strength that
faith can be in their lives.

I desired to be a coach at a very young age. The opportunity to share,
support and compete with each other in the game of football is unparalleled in
athletics, or in any other profession. My dad, Rusty Hamilton, coached many
places, including Furman and the Citadel as I went through high school. He
taught me the importance of studying the game, paying attention to detail and
caring for your players' development on and off the field. His insight beyond
the X's and O's of what it takes to be successful were and still are a positive
influence for me.

The Lord also blessed me with the greatest mother a son could ever have. My mother was loved by everyone. She was the most giving and caring person I knew. Her examples of forgiveness and unconditional love impacted me forever. I lost her to cancer in February 2000, but her influence and spirit remain with me every day. I'll never forget the Falcons' win over Notre Dame in 1996 as she battled cancer. I promised her we would win that game at Notre Dame Stadium, and thanks to the great group of players and coaches I worked with, we were able to beat the Fighting Irish 20-17 in overtime.

My family has always been such a positive influence for me. I was blessed to have Christian grandparents who were so giving and represented our family with strong character and moral values. God blessed me with a wonderful wife, Jane, who has been such an outstanding Christian role model for my children and me. Her loyalty to me through the trials of coaching means so much.

I also look back at people like Coach Bobby Ross, whom my dad worked for at the Citadel. Coach Ross' incredible work ethic, character and desire to win had such a strong influence on my beliefs regarding what a coach should be. My high school coaches, Larry Sechrist and Gary Gist, also were powerfully influential in teaching me how hard you must work to win — and win with character.

I am so appreciative of the strong, positive influences and support of my church pastors, including Ron Murray in Tennessee and Bill Lighty in Colorado. Their guiding and encouraging messages were so uplifting and inspiring to me. People like Earl Chute, Johnny Shelton and Steve McNamara, who were and are the spiritual leaders on my teams at East Tennessee State, Elon and Brevard, have impacted me in so many ways.

All of these people remain today as leaders who have the power of influence. Their character, values, work ethic and desire to do and be the right kind of people motivate me to try to do the same each day of my life, on and off the playing field.

The Air Force Academy football program had a terrific impact on my life. It wrapped up all the positive values these people gave me into one big family. We learned how to share and feel the joy of all the successes. We learned how to care and support one another through adversity. The lessons I learned at the academy have been lasting influences, teaching me how to respond to adversity in a positive manner and continue to press on in my life.

After every game, Coach DeBerry would say a few words that were so pertinent to life itself:

- "Remember who you are and what you represent." How true, because in the end, that is the legacy we all leave behind.
- "Give your parents, family, or loved ones a hug around the neck or a phone call, and let them know how much you love them," Coach said. We all understand that our parents and families helped us achieve so many accomplishments in our lives.
- "Get up on Sunday morning and go to church." Commitment to the Lord gives us the Solid Rock to always stand on and the opportunity to win the ultimate victory. I've said these words many times, as head coach, to my football teams. After one season, one of my players at East Tennessee State told me, "Coach Hamilton, thanks for all the wins we had this year, but most important, thanks for the words of wisdom that you gave us. I now know what you meant and what life is truly about."

CHAPTER TWENTY-FOUR

COL. DAVE HLATKY

Guard
Three-year letterman (1986–88)
Graduated in 1989
Hometown: Dillsburg, Pa.
Resides now: Panama City, Fla.

DAVE PLAYED A KEY ROLE AS A PUNISHING BLOCKER IN OUR RUNNING
GAME, AND WE ALWAYS RANKED AMONG THE NATIONAL LEADERS IN
RUSHING. DAVE INITIALLY SIGNED WITH A SCHOOL THAT'S NOW IN THE BIG
12 CONFERENCE, BUT A MONTH AND A HALF AFTER NATIONAL SIGNING DAY
THAT YEAR, I GOT A CALL FROM HIM. DAVE SAID, "COACH, WHY SHOULD
I GO TO THE SECOND BEST AERONAUTICAL ENGINEERING SCHOOL IN THE
COUNTRY WHEN I CAN GO TO THE BEST? CAN I STILL COME TO THE AIR
FORCE ACADEMY?" I ASSURED HIM THE OPPORTUNITY WAS STILL AVAILABLE.
DAVE WAS SINCERE ABOUT HIS EDUCATION BEING HIS TOP PRIORITY. BUT
HE ALSO WANTED TO BE A FINE COLLEGE FOOTBALL PLAYER AND TO BE A

GREAT PILOT. HE MADE ALL OF IT HAPPEN. TODAY HE'S HAVING A GREAT
CAREER AS A COMMANDER AND IS A GREAT FIGHTER PILOT.

———

Trying to define Coach DeBerry's influence on a player's life is almost as difficult
as trying to define the impact of a wonderful father on his son's life. It's almost
easier to ask, "What *didn't* he impact?" I once told Ken Rucker, the Air Force
assistant coach who recruited me, "With the exception of my wife and kids, I
owe everything good in my life to Falcon football." The more I think about it,
the more I realize my wife and kids see a little of Coach DeBerry in me every day.
Coach DeBerry, Coach Rucker and my father are my best role models for how to
be a Christian, a gentleman, a husband, a father and a friend.

The kid who left my house on July 5, 1985, already had a strong sense of
faith, family and integrity. The officer who proudly graduated from the Air Force
Academy four years later added work ethic, service to team goals and an unrelenting
commitment to never letting his brothers down. Today the 40-year-old man and
F-16 Fighting Falcon pilot at Florida's Tyndall Air Force Base reflecting on Coach
DeBerry's influence is grateful for his continued friendship with Fisher and Lu Ann.

This friendship began the day Fisher and Coach Rucker visited my family's
home during my senior year of high school. After a few minutes of pleasantries,
Coach made his sales pitch:

> David, all I can promise you is I will work your butt off. If you
> come to the Air Force Academy and play football, you will have the
> opportunity to play at the major college level against Army, Navy,
> Notre Dame and BYU, among others. You will get the opportunity to
> play in a bowl game. But more importantly, you will graduate with the
> best college degree in America, and you will get the opportunity to fly
> fighter jets and try to be the astronaut I know you want to be. But it
> won't be easy, David ... and you seem awfully big to be an astronaut.

The next fall, I began the academy's grueling 50-pound weight-loss program,
better known as basic cadet training. At first, it was football practice agony on top of
freshman hazing. But as we moved through that 1985 season, it became obvious that
the harder we worked, the better the varsity team was prepared on Saturday. That
year, Air Force was ranked as high as No. 4 in the national polls after a 10-0 start. The
Falcons shared the Western Athletic Conference championship, beat Texas 24-16 in
the Bluebonnet Bowl in Houston, finished 12-1 and led the nation in victories.

Coach DeBerry had a knack for showing up at just the right time to get our scout team fired up to dig just a little deeper. He took the time to come around and thank the scouts for keeping the pressure on and preparing *our* team for Saturday. Halfway through the season, hard work became ingrained as a fact of life.

At the same time, each practice ended with a long pep talk timed in DeBerry minutes. Those long chats covered the gamut of football, life and liberty, and player comparisons to the athletic prowess of Coach DeBerry's grandma. They also stressed teamwork and defining success as being on the scoreboard, not on an individual player's stat sheet.

Those talks were a play-by-play of everything that mattered to success. It didn't matter who carried the ball. Whoever had it was going to gain yards, and we were going to score points if everyone did his job well. This applied to the defense, special teams and the scout team as well; selflessness would enable the Falcons to succeed. As each of us internalized his part, it became easy to find pride in our success on the scoreboard.

As Coach taught us to work hard and to selflessly do our part, he also stressed never letting our brother, our teammate, down. Even when we were spent and sure that we had nothing left to give, Coach DeBerry made us know that each guy holding a hand in that huddle was feeling the exact same pain. If we couldn't find it in ourselves, we could find strength in knowing that our brothers weren't going to let us down. We owed it to our brothers to perform in kind. Our belief in and practice of this brotherhood carries on today.

Today my teammates remain my closest friends. I put the world on hold to make time for even the shortest visits. And all the "little brothers," the Air Force players who graduated after me, get looked after as well. My brothers' families are my family, and my family is theirs. In combat, nothing else compares to the trust and confidence you have flying with one of your brothers.

Twenty-three years after arriving at the Air Force Academy for the first time, I find it amazing that Fisher DeBerry, a man who never knew his own father, could be such a wonderful father figure to us and such an amazing father to Joe and Michelle, his children. It's even more amazing that a man with no brothers taught his players how to be just that, true brothers. The question isn't, "How has Coach DeBerry influenced my life?" The real question is, "What would my life be like if I hadn't played football for Coach DeBerry?" I thank God I don't have to answer that.

CHAPTER TWENTY-FIVE

LT. COL. BRIAN HILL

————

Linebacker
Three-year letterman (1988–90)
Graduated in 1991
Hometown: Columbus, Ohio
Resides now: Honolulu

————

EVERYBODY THOUGHT BRIAN WAS TOO SMALL TO PLAY DIVISION I-A FOOTBALL. EVERYBODY, THAT IS, EXCEPT BRIAN. IT DIDN'T TAKE ME LONG TO REALIZE HE WAS GOING TO BE A FINE PLAYER. HE SEEMED TO MAKE EVERY TACKLE DURING SCRIMMAGES AGAINST THE VARSITY OFFENSE. BRIAN ALSO HAD BEEN AROUND SOME PRETTY GOOD FOOTBALL AT OHIO STATE, WHERE HIS FATHER WAS THE HEAD TRAINER. BRIAN WAS VOTED THE DEFENSIVE MVP IN OUR LIBERTY BOWL VICTORY OVER OHIO STATE, WHERE HIS FATHER PRESENTED HIM THE AWARD. THAT WAS A REAL THRILL FOR BOTH OF THEM. BRIAN IS POTENTIALLY ONE OF THE BEST COACHING CANDIDATES I HAVE EVER BEEN AROUND. HE HAS SO MUCH TO OFFER PLAYERS, AND I HOPE HE GETS THAT OPPORTUNITY SOMEDAY.

————

"No thanks, Coach."

After four years of answering every Fisher DeBerry request with a hearty and sincere yes, I had turned Coach down. Yes, Coach, I will keep my feet moving through the tackle. Yes, I will study game film every night. Yes, I will split the guard-tackle double team and hold my ground in the hole. Yes, I will commit 110 percent to the offseason strength and conditioning program. Yes, I will remember who I am in the squadron, the classroom and the community. Yes, I will try to call my mother and father each Sunday and let them know I appreciate their support and sacrifices. Yes, I will embrace this sacred and special brotherhood that is Falcon Football and let it guide my growth and development at the academy and beyond. Yet all I said to Coach DeBerry's personal offer to work at the Air Force Prep School as a teacher, coach and assistant athletic director was "No thanks."

Four years of saying yes to Coach DeBerry had turned out just fine for me. I was a three-year starter after walking on to the team in 1987. I was a proud member of three Commander-in-Chief's Trophy-winning teams. I played in two Liberty Bowls, including a 23-11 upset victory in 1990 over my beloved Ohio State Buckeyes, whose head trainer happened to be my father, Billy. I was selected a team captain and MVP. Most important, I gained 19 brothers whom I sweated with, bled with, laughed with and cried with — 19 brothers who taught me the true meaning of the whole always being greater than its individual parts.

To this day, I believe that divine intervention kept me from making the biggest of mistakes by declining Coach DeBerry's offer. Refusing to give up, Coach DeBerry energetically asked me, "Brian, have you talked to your daddy about this offer yet?" To which I replied, "No, I haven't."

After talking to my father and a few senior Air Force officers, I am glad to say I accepted Coach DeBerry's offer to return to the academy and join Denny Moore (AFA Class of 1983) and the prep-school staff.

Coaching football at the Air Force Prep School was about much more than X's and O's. Thankfully, I came to understand that the tools our players needed to succeed at the Air Force Academy were not centered on their mastery of the Falcons' playbook and how to execute "Right 34-5" or "4-Okie Shoot," but more on the strong principles Fisher DeBerry used to build the Falcon Football program so well:

- "The only place where success comes before work is in the dictionary;"
- "The players need to know how much you care before they will care how much you know."
- "Brothers are hard to beat."

We played football from August until October at the prep school. In the seven months that remained until our preppies graduated, we interacted with them in areas outside of athletics to keep them motivated and focused on staying with us and earning their appointments to the Air Force Academy. To do this, we carried the messages of Coach DeBerry and the rest of his staff on a daily basis, because the prep school players' contact with the AFA staff was limited by NCAA regulations.

We not only worked hard to keep our student-athletes focused on the goal of accepting appointments to the Air Force Academy, there were approximately 170 other cadet candidates at the prep school, and we believed our mission of leadership, guidance, mentorship and instruction included them as well. In keeping with Coach DeBerry's all-important principle that family formed the foundation of the Falcons' success, Suzette, my new bride at the time (and now my wife of more than 15 years), embraced the Air Force Prep School experience by serving as a volunteer assistant women's basketball coach. She also ensured that our home was open to any preppie who needed a home-cooked meal or a place to decompress on a free weekend.

Today's college football landscape measures program success in wins achieved in the shortest amount of time. Our vision for success took on a long-range outlook as we reinforced Coach DeBerry's principles of hard work, perseverance and overcoming adversity. We had a unique situation at the prep school because our students' achievements wouldn't be gauged for two or three years, after they had moved on to the Air Force Academy as cadet-athletes.

As a football coach, I take great pride that our two classes went 22-4 as juniors and seniors with the Falcons in 1997 and 1998, including an outright Western Athletic Conference championship, the greatest two-year run in Air Force football history. As an Air Force officer, I am confident these former preppies and cadets make our officer corps the best it has been in the Air Force's grand history of 60-plus years. Coach DeBerry's legacy extends far beyond the gridiron and significantly contributes to our nation's security.

I often thought about how best to pay back Coach DeBerry for his inspirational leadership and influence in my life. "You can never pay back, but you can always pay forward," said the late Woody Hayes, legendary football coach at Ohio State and a childhood hero of mine. If great people have done good things for you, you really can't pay them back, but you can pay the good things forward by sharing those lessons and principles with others you come in contact with throughout your life.

As former Air Force football players, we pay forward every time we quote Coach DeBerry to our families, co-workers and communities. Coach DeBerry's principles for football, life and right living are timeless lessons that are sure to be shared and appreciated for generations to come.

Thank you, Coach.

CHAPTER TWENTY-SIX

TIM HORTON

Receivers coach (1999–2004)
Halfbacks coach (2005)
Hometown: Conway, Ark.
Resides now: Fayetteville, Ark.

TIM IS ON A FAST TRACK TO BECOME ONE OF THE NATION'S PREMIER HEAD COACHES. I PREDICT TIM WILL SOON BE A HEAD COACH AT ONE OF OUR NATION'S TOP COLLEGE FOOTBALL PROGRAMS. NOT ONLY IS TIM A WONDERFUL COACH, HE'S ONE OF THE BEST HUMAN BEINGS I'VE EVER KNOWN. HIS CHARACTER AND PERSONAL QUALITIES MAKE HIM THE KIND OF COACH WE WOULD ALL WANT OUR SONS TO PLAY FOR.

Coach DeBerry and Ronald Reagan rank as the master communicators in my mind. If 10 letters came into Coach DeBerry's office, you could be sure 10 responses would go out. Kathy Shipley was the perfect administrative assistant for Coach DeBerry — she was one of the few who could read his writing! He was also outstanding on the telephone with high school recruits and their parents and coaches, tirelessly recruiting almost nightly during an NCAA-allowed contact period. Yet Coach DeBerry communicated most powerfully through his behavior and service-driven actions.

As the running backs and tight-ends coach and recruiting coordinator at my alma mater, the University of Arkansas at Fayetteville, I make it a point each day to apply a lesson learned from Coach DeBerry. The first quality of great character is honesty. Coach DeBerry required each Air Force assistant to have individual position meetings with every player, where we talked about the player's strengths and weaknesses and where he stood on the depth chart. "Be completely honest with every player we are entrusted with," Coach DeBerry would say.

I believe a person's best sermon is what you see, not what you hear. With Coach DeBerry, you see his faith in his daily life. When I was coaching for him, he never missed a Wednesday morning staff Bible study, the team's "share time" the night before a game, a Friday morning Bible study at the Radisson Inn near the south gate of the academy, or sitting in his favorite west-side pew at Sunrise United Methodist Church on Sunday morning. He had the same consistency as a husband, father, coach, friend and mentor.

Lu Ann DeBerry, a remarkably wonderful person as well, is a first-class lady. I don't know of a better role model for so many coaches' wives. The coaching profession is tough on coaches' wives because of our long hours of work and all the time we're away from home. Believe me, it takes a very special, understanding person to be a coach's wife. I know for my wife, Lauren, Lu Ann always will be the gold standard.

Coach DeBerry always impressed me with his extraordinary willingness to go to bat for kids. Whenever a cadet faced any adversity at the academy, Coach DeBerry always provided full support and what I call "stick up." It didn't matter whether the cadet involved was a first-team player or a fifth-team player on the football squad; Coach DeBerry stood by his side.

There are 18,000 acres of beautiful land at the Air Force Academy, and I treasure the many miles of jogging with Coach DeBerry around the vast athletic fields. I would ask question after question, and Coach always answered with great wisdom. I asked him about his playing days at Wofford College, about his coaching roots at Wofford, about coaching at Appalachian State University, and about his six seasons coaching in the South Carolina high school ranks. As former staff mate Jappy Oliver would say, "This is the best job we will ever have."

Recruiting with Fisher was a joy. First, he paid for every meal. Second, he loved to visit with student-athletes and their parents. He enjoyed recruiting in the warm-weather areas of the country the most — it was in his beloved Cheraw, S.C., blood. In fact, longtime assistant coach Dick Enga often told a funny story of how Coach DeBerry about froze to death during a mid-January recruiting trip to Minnesota — and never went back.

Coach DeBerry said, "You will become who and what you associate yourself with." Whenever I think of the men I want to emulate, I quickly think of Coach DeBerry and former Air Force assistants Bob Noblitt, Dean Campbell, Richard Bell and Chuck Petersen, as well as staff members Troy Garnhart and Jim Bowman, among so many others.

In Coach DeBerry's office hung a wooden sign with the words: "Make the big time where you are." Coach DeBerry did just that by making Air Force football big time.

CHAPTER TWENTY-SEVEN

CAPT. JACKSON WHITING

———

Kicker
Three-year letterman (1997–99)
Graduated in 2000
Hometown: Columbia, S.C.
Resides now: Panama City, Fla.

———

JACKSON WAS JUST AS ACCURATE AS THE TRUTH. AS A SENIOR IN 1999, HE HAD THE ONLY PERFECT SEASON BY A KICKER IN AIR FORCE HISTORY. HE SET ANOTHER SCHOOL RECORD BY GOING 19 FOR 23 ON FIELD GOALS FOR HIS CAREER (82.6 PERCENT). WHEN YOUR KICKER IS THAT ACCURATE, YOU SLEEP A LOT BETTER IF YOU'RE A COACH. TODAY, JACKSON IS HAVING QUITE A CAREER AS AN AIR FORCE PILOT. OF COURSE, I'M NOT SURPRISED. HE WAS ALWAYS IN SUCH CONTROL DURING TIGHT GAME SITUATIONS. JACKSON DEVELOPED SO MUCH CONFIDENCE IN HIS ABILITY AS A KICKER, NOT ONCE DID I GIVE A SECOND THOUGHT TO CALLING ON HIM TO GO WIN A GAME FOR US.

———

Anxiety hit hard and threatened to overcome me during the three weeks before my first actual football game with the Air Force varsity team. The anxiety started soon after Maj. Jeff Hays, my terrific position coach, told me that I would be the Falcons' starting field-goal kicker for the 1998 season, my junior year. I had traveled with the varsity squad my entire sophomore season, but I had never stepped foot on the field. Other than kicking in warm-ups before the games that year, I stayed on the sideline, watching and learning. Now it was my turn to contribute.

But kicking in front of 55,000 screaming fans was something I had never experienced. How would I react? Would I step up to the challenge? Or would I falter when the time came to perform? These thoughts ran through my head leading up to our 1998 season opener against Wake Forest at Falcon Stadium. We were coming off a 10-3 season that included a 7-0 start and a year-ending trip to the Las Vegas Bowl, and we had high hopes for similar, if not better success in 1998.

Now when I look back on my Air Force Academy experience, I realize that playing Falcon football is where I learned the two most important lessons that have carried me through my career as an F-15 Eagle pilot and in my life when I'm not flying: Trust in God and your teammates, and mentally prepare for success.

For three consecutive weeks before that 1998 opener, my mind was racing. Academically, I was taking 21 hours that semester with a heavy load of difficult mechanical engineering classes. I couldn't afford not to listen to my professors in class, yet I couldn't take my mind off our season opener. Though I was confident in my physical ability to kick a football, I was unsure how I would react mentally.

Looking back, I realize the genius behind good coaching is mentally preparing your team to win. Before you can properly train physically, you must have the right mental mind-set. Coach DeBerry taught us how to win by teaching us how to prepare our minds for battle as we physically trained to fight. At the end of each practice, he would motivate us with a story or "DeBerryism" that related back to our ability to succeed as a team.

Usually his analogies involved humor, such as this DeBerryism: "If you ever see a turtle sitting on a fence post, you can be sure he didn't get there by himself." To this day, I've never seen a turtle on a fence post, but that analogy speaks volumes about Air Force football. We came to understand that as individuals, we could not achieve our goals, but together, we would achieve the unthinkable as a team. This mentality drove our work ethic. We had to trust that every player was giving his all on and off the field, because that's what was required to win. We didn't do anything by ourselves. Accountability was the only way to ensure we gave all we had.

Accountability was especially important in the summer when school was out. Unlike other major college football players, cadets at the Air Force Academy get only three weeks of leave every summer, and the rest of their time is spent in various programs at the academy or out in the active-duty Air Force.

The summer before my junior year, I spent three weeks at Andrews Air Force Base near Washington in a program called Operations Air Force. During this time, of the 15 or so cadets who participated at Andrews, Craig Thorstenson, our middle linebacker, and I were the only two football players. Kickers and middle linebackers don't usually partner up in the weight room. But I remember thinking to myself (and I know he thought the same): "I am the only person who will push Craig for three weeks while we are here at Andrews. His ability to train and get better will be directly related to how much I push myself, and how much I push him." There was an unspoken trust that we wouldn't let each other down. During those three weeks, we trained together both in the weight room and on the field. It was obvious why kickers and middle linebackers don't work out together, because I spent a good bit of time just removing weights. But it didn't matter. We were going to make each other better.

As a kicker, I learned that trust in God was my only way to truly sleep at night, because I realized I really couldn't do it on my own. The pressure didn't come from friends, family members or fans; I experienced self-induced pressure because I didn't want to let my teammates down. Guys who had given everything they had for the team needed me to succeed the rare times I stepped onto the field so that we could win football games.

After struggling with this mounting pressure, I knew the only way I could mentally prepare was to give my efforts to God and let Him use me in accordance with His plan. God had a plan for me, whether that plan involved me falling on my face after my first kick or enjoying a successful football season. His plan was perfect, and it had a purpose. There were many times when I failed to trust in God and tried to do things on my own, but God truly is faithful and always brought me back.

With the help of God, first and foremost, and the teaching of Coach Hays, mental preparation became the key to my success as a kicker. The most important thing Coach Hays taught me was to see myself executing perfectly in my mind every day, and to purposefully think through that execution in vivid detail. Not once did I ever see myself making a mistake. I built confidence in my ability to execute perfectly regardless of the situation. I learned that the majority of pressure is self-generated. Unnecessary stress will hinder performance, and it is imperative to eliminate it through proper focus and mental preparation. This more than anything else will lead to consistent execution.

Air Force football taught me that giving my efforts to God is the only way to remove the massive internal and external pressures we face on a daily basis in life. Additionally, I learned that mental preparation will fine-tune my abilities, enabling me to consistently perform under any conditions. These two principles guided me through intense Air Force pilot training — from my first flight in a Cessna to my last flight in an F-15C instructor pilot upgrade.

Now with the 95th Fighter Squadron at Tyndall Air Force Base in Florida, I have proudly served in the Air Force more than eight years. I have sat "Alert" and flown Homeland Defense missions here in the United States, and I'm working toward my MBA from the University of Florida while continuing to serve as an F-15C instructor pilot.

During my junior season in 1998, the year we went 12-1 and won the Western Athletic Conference championship, I converted 53 of 54 extra-point attempts and kicked seven field goals. I never missed during my senior year in 1999, going 12 of 12 on field goals and 26 of 26 on extra points. After all that worrying early on, my Air Force football career turned out to be a real kick.

Chapter Twenty-Eight

NATE BEARD

Fullback
Two-year letterman (1999–2000)
Graduated in 2001
Hometown: Grand Junction, Colo.
Resides now: Grand Junction, Colo.

WE HIT A HOME RUN BY HAVING NATE PLAY FULLBACK FOR US. NATE WAS FROM COLORADO, AND, MAN, DID HE TAKE ENORMOUS PRIDE IN PLAYING FOR THE BLUE AND SILVER AND WEARING OUR FAMED LIGHTNING BOLTS ON HIS HELMET. NATE WAS ONE OF THE MOST INTENSE PLAYERS I HAVE EVER BEEN AROUND. AND HE WORKED SO HARD IN THE WEIGHT ROOM, WE BROUGHT HIM BACK TO THE ACADEMY AS A STRENGTH COACH BECAUSE OF THE INFLUENCE WE KNEW HE WOULD HAVE ON OUR YOUNGER PLAYERS. NATE ALSO MARRIED THE SISTER OF A TEAMMATE. THAT SHOULD TELL YOU A LOT ABOUT THE GREAT RESPECT PEOPLE HAD FOR NATE.

Next to my parents, I credit Air Force football as the most important factor in making me who I am today. I often struggled while attending the academy, and my time on the practice field wasn't any easier. Competition was fierce, setbacks were inevitable and the coaches always were watching and critiquing every action. I spent most of my first two years struggling to make the varsity team. There were times I thought I might get cut, and other times I felt I was only one play away from being a starter. During those first two years, I became callous to the emotional setbacks and learned to keep my eyes focused on my goal of playing and being a starter on the varsity squad.

During a post-practice speech during my sophomore year, Coach DeBerry told us that he always knew where to find Chris Gizzi or Beau Morgan when he was looking for them. They were always in the weight room making themselves better. Gizzi was one of the best linebackers in Air Force history, and Morgan was one of the best quarterbacks the Falcons ever produced. They were two athletes who enjoyed tremendous success at the academy, and Coach DeBerry reminded us that they worked for and earned that success. After that speech, there was never a free minute when I wasn't in the weight room.

I am a big believer that football is a combination of preparation and opportunity. In any given practice or game, there may be only one play that will catch the coach's eye or ensure a victory for your team. If you haven't done everything possible to prepare to succeed on that play, your opportunity for success will pass you by. Some athletes never prepare, and others are never given the opportunity. If I didn't become a starter for the Air Force varsity, it wasn't going to be because I failed to prepare.

My junior and senior years had their share of adversity, but my commitment to success began to pay off. The start of my junior season, I stood on the sideline as our third-string fullback. I had done everything I could to prepare, and I was eagerly waiting for my opportunity. With only minutes left in a close game against the Washington Huskies in Seattle, our second game that year, Coach DeBerry put me in. I'm sure it was because he needed some fresh legs in there, but I also knew this was the opportunity I had been working and waiting for. The stadium was so loud, I couldn't hear our quarterback making calls at the line of scrimmage. All I could do was watch for the snap of the ball. I tried to hold back the adrenaline and the anticipation of the snap, but I jumped offside. A penalty was the last thing the Falcons needed at that time. I was worried that I had just blown my big opportunity, but Coach DeBerry left me in.

On the next play, the crowd was just as loud, but I knew what to expect. It was a triple-option play to the right side of our formation. As the center snapped the ball, I took my steps exactly as practiced. I went through my mesh with the quarterback and discovered he had given me the ball. I made one cut at linebacker level and carried the Washington free safety on my back for 15 more yards. I had the fresh legs Coach DeBerry was hoping for. He gave me the ball the next eight plays until we had run the clock down enough to ensure a 31-21 victory. I had prepared for my opportunity, and it had paid off. My total time on the field was less than five minutes, but that playing time changed my life forever. For the next two years, I played or started in every game.

I ended up being selected as a team co-captain in 2000, my senior season. That honor meant the world to me, as did receiving the Brian Bullard Memorial Award following my senior season. That prestigious team award is based on unselfishness, effort, commitment to the Falcons and pride in your role, whether you're a starter or a backup player. I was proud to receive it and pleased to know that others within the program recognized just how important Air Force football was, and still is, to me.

Life after playing for Fisher DeBerry and the Falcons has changed, but not to a great extent. The bruises and setbacks that football dished out are no different from the setbacks I have experienced in my career after football. When the chips are stacked against me, I reflect on my challenging time at the academy. Starting a business, building a house and raising kids are difficult tasks — the whole world seems to be your competition. When things get tough, I joke with my wife that we are simply reliving my first two years at the Air Force Academy. If we keep our heads up and our legs driving, things will get better, and success will be inevitable. It will be only a matter of time, and we will get our opportunity, just like I did during that 1999 game against Washington.

If I were to credit anyone for most influencing my life, it would be all my brothers on the Air Force football team. Coach DeBerry's leadership and motivation, Chris Gizzi's humility, Scott Becker's work ethic, Mike Gallagher's passion, Scotty McKay's assurance and Mike Thiessen's poise had a tremendous impact on my life. We all became so close during those years, we formed relationships like brothers.

I took our Air Force football brotherhood one step further in 2002 and married Ashlee, the sister of Ryan Fleming, our star wide receiver. Ashlee and I enjoy a tremendous relationship together and now have two little Falcons, Olivia and Braxton. We credit Air Force football for everything we have and look forward to doing everything we can to support the program under Troy Calhoun's leadership.

I separated from the Air Force in September 2007 and partnered with a seasoned engineer in a small two-man engineering and consulting company in western Colorado. I still have dreams of Coach DeBerry calling me to say that the Air Force Falcons just realized I have one more year of eligibility.

CHAPTER TWENTY-NINE

LT. COL. STEVE SENN (RET.)

Wide receiver
Three-year letterman (1987–89)
Graduated in 1990
Junior-varsity head coach, varsity assistant (2005–08)
Hometown: Albuquerque, N.M.
Resides now: Colorado Springs, Colo.

STEVE GREW UP IN A MILITARY FAMILY, SO HE KNEW HOW TO DO THINGS THE RIGHT WAY. STEVE ALWAYS WENT FULL THROTTLE AND MADE A GREAT COMPETITOR. HE WAS A GREAT RECEIVER IN AN OFFENSE THAT PROBABLY DIDN'T PASS THE BALL ENOUGH. BUT WE THREW MORE THAN MOST TRIPLE-OPTION TEAMS, AND THAT'S PRIMARILY BECAUSE STEVE CAUGHT EVERYTHING THAT CAME HIS WAY. HE HAD A SPECTACULAR SENIOR SEASON IN 1989, AVERAGING 19.5 YARDS ON 30 RECEPTIONS. STEVE ALSO HAD A GREAT CAREER AS AN AIR FORCE PILOT, FLYING GENERAL OFFICERS ALL OVER THE WORLD. I BROUGHT HIM BACK TO THE ACADEMY TO COACH

BECAUSE I KNEW HE WOULD HAVE SUCH A POSITIVE INFLUENCE ON OUR
PLAYERS. HE FAR EXCEEDED MY EXPECTATIONS.

––––––––

"That's a great play! That's how you go up for the ball! You keep making plays like
that, you'll be a Fightin' Falcon real soon!"

Those are the first words I remember hearing from Coach DeBerry. It
was the fall of 1985. I was a wide receiver at the Air Force Academy Prep School,
and we were having a scrimmage on the varsity team's practice fields. I had just
made a catch in the end zone over a defensive back. Coach DeBerry ran up to me
while I was on my back with the ball in my hands and uttered those words in his
wonderful South Carolina drawl. That was my first face-to-face encounter with the
Air Force head coach, who would have a great impact on my 20 years of service in
the Air Force.

Influence, faith and adversity are unusual words in a young man's
vocabulary. But as a 5-foot-10, 150-pound prospect from Albuquerque, I didn't
have any Division I-A schools offering me a football scholarship. Even though I
was an all-state quarterback and free safety in high school, New Mexico wasn't
known for being a recruiting hotbed of major college talent. My first step into the
world of Air Force football began when my mother asked me whether it would be
OK if she submitted a questionnaire to the Air Force Academy on my behalf. As a
high school senior, I wasn't very proactive about my future, but my mother knew
exactly what she was doing. Bob Noblitt, the offensive coordinator on Coach
DeBerry's staff at Air Force, visited our home, and he offered me a "scholarship"
to the prep school.[1] Coach DeBerry had just completed his first year as the head
coach at the Air Force Academy. As I look back on my early years at the prep
school and at the academy, I came to realize how all three qualities – influence,
faith and adversity – played a central role in my life in the years to follow.

By far, the biggest influences in my life are my parents. My father is a retired
enlisted man with a long career of devoted military service. He left L.A. (Lower
Alabama) at age 18 to pursue a better life in the Air Force. He didn't come from
much, but he ended up with a lot.

Dad spent 28 years in the Air Force and taught me to always give

––––––––––––––––––

1. Cadets enroll at the Air Force Academy with congressional appointments. Students enroll at the Air Force
   Academy Prep School with the goal of qualifying for admittance to the Air Force Academy. When Steve Senn refers
   to his "scholarship," it's his way of saying that he was guided to the prep school by the AFA coaching staff in hopes
   that he would qualify for entry into the academy one year later.

it my best, because great things would happen if I did. He taught me the fundamentals of all sports: football — baseball, basketball, golf and more. He played high school football and had great speed, which he handed down to his son. He started me playing football in Young America Football League when I was only 8, and I truly believe I eventually was able to play at the major college level because I started in the game at such a young age. I learned how to take a hit, deliver a hit and, more important, be a team player.

My mother played an equally important influential role in my life. She was my den mother for Cub Scouts, booster-club president during high school and, like my father, attended every game I played for Air Force. While my father was stationed in Germany for my junior-high years, my parents procured a cowbell from a farmer in rural Switzerland. That cowbell made it to every high school game and every Air Force game of mine. Whenever I would come out at the beginning of a game, I would hear the cowbell and know exactly where to find my parents in the stands. After I would make a catch or a good block, I would hear that cowbell and just point to the sound. Knowing my parents were in the stands for every game meant a lot to me.

Coaches also played an influential role in my life, from my Pee Wee Football days with Coach Onadera, to my high school days with Coach Sewell, to my Air Force Prep School days with Coach Mastin, to my academy career with Coach DeBerry.

During my Pee Wee days, my coach primarily talked about the fundamentals of football and what it meant to keep your head up when you tackle. During high school, my coach talked more about the X's and O's of football and about being a role model for younger players. At the prep school, my coach focused on being a team player. And at the academy, Coach DeBerry taught me the ingredients of being a better man: honor, integrity and family.

I was fortunate to make the varsity team's travel roster as a freshman wide receiver for the Falcons and was able to be around Coach DeBerry on a daily basis. Every day after practice, we circled up and "took a knee" as Coach discussed the upcoming opponent and life lessons. I learned about Coach DeBerry's upbringing by his grandmother and how he had very little growing up. My father didn't have very much growing up either. That's why he enlisted in the Air Force at such a young age. Both Coach DeBerry and my father taught me to appreciate the little things in life and to be thankful for what I had. Coach DeBerry taught me not to be so proud of my individual accomplishments that I overlooked the far greater importance of always celebrating as a team. I remember him saying, "Gentlemen, just remember, there's no *I* in the letter team!"

When I had the opportunity to return to the Air Force Academy in 2002 as a military coach, I learned even more from Coach DeBerry. This time around, he showed me the importance of putting a comforting arm around a player when he was having a bad day, but to hold his feet to the fire when needed. I learned firsthand about his tremendous work ethic and what it takes to have a successful football program at the major college level.

Teammates had tremendous influence on my life as well. When you enter the Air Force Academy, you go through so much together in such a short amount of time, you really come to see your teammates as your brothers. There would be days when the academy lifestyle had me feeling down. I would come down from the hill to our team's locker room inside the Cadet Field House, and without fail, one of my teammates would quickly lift my spirits.

I roomed with quarterback Lance McDowell for three years on the varsity team. Lance was a backup to Dee Dowis, a Heisman Trophy finalist our senior year in 1989 and one of the best quarterbacks in Air Force history. Lance's attitude was always upbeat and influential. Even though Lance knew he wasn't going to get much playing time as Dee's backup, he remained positive and focused on the game. I learned a lot from Lance: No matter what life has in store for you, your positive attitude can make all the difference.

Coach DeBerry may not realize it, but he also influenced my faith. He is a deeply religious man, and not afraid to let you know it. He encouraged me to become involved with the Fellowship of Christian Athletes. FCA offered a wonderful place for athletes to openly discuss what it was like to be a Christian athlete. The biggest lesson I learned from those discussions was that as an athlete, you never knew who was watching you, so conduct yourself properly. Little kids often watched our practices, and most of my Air Force games were played in front of 40,000 or more fans and sometimes were televised nationally. So I worked to ensure my actions on the field reflected the person I was inside.

In 1989, my senior year, we were 6-0 and ranked No. 17 in the country while awaiting a visit from Notre Dame, the defending national champion. Notre Dame, 5-0 and ranked No. 1, carried a 17-game winning streak. Their visit marked the first time a top-ranked team had played at Falcon Stadium. Even though we fell behind early and eventually lost 41-27, we outscored the powerhouse Irish during the second half. We never gave up, battled adversity and fought until the last whistle. Life lessons like that have enabled me to overcome the adversities I have faced during my Air Force career.

I was stationed as a C-5 pilot at Travis Air Force Base in California when the 9/11 attacks on our country occurred. The world as we knew it changed forever. I began flying missions to Diego Garcia in the Indian Ocean following the order to attack the Taliban in Afghanistan. My mission was to take the bombs from the United States, air refuel across the Pacific Ocean and deliver them to our B-1 aircraft stationed in Diego Garcia. I would do this for the next six months. My crew of 12 had the "opportunity" to sleep in a one-bedroom house on the island of Guam. That translated to 12 cots in a one-bedroom house. I was fortunate to get the closet, so I could block out some of the snoring.

During the start of Enduring Freedom, we lost an engine immediately after taking off from Hickam Air Force Base in Hawaii. My C-5 crew determined that we had a malfunction on an outboard engine and needed to shut it down before it compounded into a much worse problem. So I made an emergency return to Hickam to land a 720,000-pound C-5 airplane on a wet runway. The "battles" I had been in at the Air Force Academy and on the football field had prepared me for this type of tense situation.

I have been very blessed throughout my life. I have had a tremendous upbringing by terrific parents. I have had the opportunity to play major college football, serve my country for more than 20 years and coach at the major college level. I have a beautiful family. The lessons I learned as an Air Force Academy cadet and as a player for Coach DeBerry have made lasting impressions on me as a husband, father, coach and officer.

CHAPTER THIRTY

DAVE HILDEBRAND

———

Guard
Three-year letterman (1998–2000)
Graduated in 2001
Hometown: Houston, Texas
Resides now: San Antonio, Texas

———

I HAD MORE FUN COACHING DAVE THAN I DID ANY OTHER PLAYER. FOR A "FAT BOY," HE WAS ONE OF THE MOST COMPETITIVE PLAYERS WE EVER HAD AT AIR FORCE. DAVE EARNED THE RIGHT TO PLAY IN THE EAST-WEST SHRINE GAME AS A SENIOR BECAUSE THERE WERE VERY FEW OFFENSIVE LINEMEN IN THE COUNTRY BETTER THAN HE WAS. HIS TEAMMATES ALWAYS THOUGHT WE WERE AT EACH OTHER, BUT THEY JUST DIDN'T KNOW THE RESPECT WE HAD FOR EACH OTHER. DAVE WAS A VERY EFFECTIVE LEADER AND HAD REAL POSITIVE INFLUENCE ON HIS TEAM. HE WAS A HUGE FACTOR IN THE FALCONS AVERAGING NEARLY 35 POINTS AND NEARLY 300 YARDS RUSHING PER GAME IN 2000, HIS SENIOR SEASON.

———

Playing football at the Air Force Academy is the pinnacle of any football experience, pro or college. After completing my AFA career, I had the opportunity to play in the prestigious East-West Shrine all-star game in San Francisco. The year I played, the great players included linemen Leonard Davis and Casey Hampton and wide receivers T.J. Houshmandzadeh and Steve Smith. I was a late invitee and felt very fortunate to be included in a group of such talented athletes. For most of the prospective NFL players, it was a weeklong interview process in a very competitive and sometimes stressful environment. I held little hope of becoming an NFL player at that time, so I soaked in the experience and observed those around me who aspired to become NFL stars — yet they didn't impress me. These guys focused on making themselves look good so they could receive a bigger paycheck. After experiencing the polar opposite of playing for Fisher DeBerry and the Falcons, it repulsed me.

When we played in big games at Air Force — and we played in many, for conference championships and in bowl games — I could not have cared less about winning for myself. I wanted to play my butt off so my best friends could put a championship ring on their finger and have the bragging rights of winning bowl games. (Navy was an exception. That was personal.) I doubt I will experience the same camaraderie again.

The biggest influence in my life was my high school football coach Mike Hall. I played at Second Baptist High School in Houston when the football program had been in existence for only six years. Coach Hall's background was women's soccer, so at the time he was no disciple of football X's and O's. But Coach Hall was an extremely solid guy to play for. He genuinely cared for me and my teammates. There never was a single instance that triggered my love for Coach Hall, but his influence spread as he lived his day-to-day life. He was a coach who exuded faith, integrity and self-discipline in his daily interactions with his family and players. He was an extraordinary example of the kind of Christian man I wanted to be.

When I played for Coach Hall, I learned who I wanted to become, where I wanted to go and how I wanted to accomplish my goals. Not only was Coach Hall an influence in my life, but the entire Second Baptist football coaching staff was as well. One assistant coach eventually became an ordained minister and was the minister who performed my wedding ceremony seven years after I graduated from high school.

Then there was Coach DeBerry, master of the profoundly dumb statement. (I mean that in the nicest way.) He started many after-practice team speeches by saying something incredibly stupid, and for good reason. He purposely let a few seconds pass to allow us to think about the nonsense that had just exited his mouth. We would look around at each other, in amazement that Coach DeBerry had, yet again, "out-dumbed" himself. He continued with a smirk on his face, and "99 times out of 10," he turned his lunacy into something remarkably profound.

Whether anyone was aware of it or not (including Coach DeBerry himself), I think lunacy was the master strategy he used to grab our attention and keep us focused on his message. One example of his message-within-a-story technique featured a turtle. In the midst of the West Texas desert, DeBerry saw something strange on top of a fence post. A turtle laid tummy-side up, legs stretching into the sky. "That turtle didn't get there by himself," Coach DeBerry would say. *"Ask your teammate for help!"*

Coach DeBerry should win an award as the Cliché Coach. I wish I had kept track of these "DeBerryisms." A few of my favorites include: "Am I smoking smoke?" "Eat till it ouches you!" "You guys are skating on thin water"; "You're moving as fast as Methuselah"; "You've gotta twist the dagger!"

I don't recall any specific game of my Air Force career as the most memorable. But what still sticks out is a tradition I developed with Coach DeBerry during every game of my senior year. I was an offensive lineman, and because of our triple-option offense, many AFA linemen were skinnier than offensive linemen at most schools. I was an exception; during my playing years, I had a big belly. After touchdown drives, Coach DeBerry would run up to me, jump and throw his belly into mine. This belly bump became our thing. We did it after every touchdown, and we did it off the field, too. I think it was his way of saying to the players, "See, fellas, I'm hip, I'm cool. I can bump bellies with the biggest bellies of them all." Our belly bump became part of his grand scheme of leadership by lunacy.

Now I work in corporate America for Valero Energy at the company's headquarters in San Antonio. Many values I gained from the military and college football extend into corporate life.

- Team—You're always going to work in a team. Sometimes you might be the leader. Other times, you might be a follower. Either way, you gain experience. To be a leader, you must first learn how to be a good follower.
- Intelligence—By my count, 95 out of 100 Air Force Academy graduates are intelligent. The other five are flying F-15s. And those five are buddies of mine, so trust me when I say I am serious. Don't ask me how they became pilots. They obviously had more of the next trait I name.

- Self-discipline (hard work)—There are always people out there who work harder than you. They are called soldiers. I'm not a soldier at heart, but I learned a lot about how hard they work while I was one. I wish more corporate employees spent time in the military to learn this trait.
- Time management—Simply put, if you want to survive as a cadet, you learn to master this at the Air Force Academy. The same applies in the corporate world.
- Integrity—I developed this virtue before I became a cadet. The Air Force Academy will give you a million dollars worth of integrity training, one nickel at a time.

I have been married almost five years and have one precious 19-month-old boy and a baby girl due. It's always been my dream to be the Christian leader of my family and a solid father and husband. The Lord has blessed me with a wonderful wife. So things have worked out very well for me, just as I desired.

When you're talking about the right kind of influence, I think of people who share my values — faith and family — and vital virtues such as wisdom and self-discipline. You simply can't go wrong when you apply any of those to your life, on or off the football field.

Chapter Thirty-One

DEAN CAMPBELL

Running backs coach (2000–04)
Secondary coach (2005–06)
Hometown: Austin, Texas
Resides now: Fayetteville, Ark.

AFTER PLAYING ON TWO NATIONAL CHAMPIONSHIP TEAMS AT TEXAS, DEAN WAS DESTINED TO HAVE A GREAT COACHING CAREER. HE'S HAD EXACTLY THAT. WE MET AT A FELLOWSHIP OF CHRISTIAN ATHLETES CONFERENCE, AND WE BOTH FELT WE NEEDED TO COACH TOGETHER SOMEDAY BECAUSE OF OUR SIMILAR BELIEFS, PHILOSOPHIES AND VALUES, AND THE RESPECT WE HAD FOR EACH OTHER'S FAMILIES. DEAN IS ONE OF THE MOST LOYAL PEOPLE I HAVE EVER KNOWN, AND THE KIND OF PERSON AND COACH I WOULD ASPIRE TO BE IF I WERE BEGINNING TO COACH TODAY.

I first met Fisher and Lu Ann DeBerry at a Fellowship of Christian Athletes coaches conference in 1984 in Colorado, and all these years later, I still have the notes from Coach DeBerry's lecture when he spoke to us about the priorities in his life: faith, family and Air Force Falcons football, in that order. He still believed very strongly in those priorities when we were coaching together in 2006, in what turned out to be his final season at the academy.

Ever since we met Fisher and Lu Ann, my wife, Cindy, and I have remained close friends with them. We had met twice in bowl games as opponents and always enjoyed visiting each year at the national coaches convention. Coaching with Fisher at the Air Force Academy became a goal for me. In a profession that pressures you to win at all costs, here was a man of strong faith and character. Getting an opportunity to coach at Air Force didn't appear likely to ever happen because openings on Fisher's staff were so rare. But in December 1999, Todd Bynum left the staff, and I jumped at the opportunity to join Fisher at the academy.

In our seven years at the academy, we experienced all the highs and lows that come with the coaching profession. The one thing I will remember most about Fisher is the way he handled both of them: the same. He emphasized that you don't panic during hard times and that you don't get too satisfied when things are going well. Coach the players hard, but be fair. Push them to be the best they can be. Get them to believe they can beat anybody in the country.

Fisher truly believed we were coaching the most talented young men in the United States — and they were. Maybe not in terms of football talent, but definitely in more important terms of character, intelligence, attitude, work ethic, heart, dedication, desire and the will to persevere, no matter the odds. That's what Fisher's Falcons were made of during his 23 years as Air Force's head coach, and I am grateful I was able to see it and experience it firsthand.

Fisher believed our job as a coaching staff was to help our players grow and become as strong as they could be in academics, athletics and their faith. He was, and remains today, a tremendous Christian role model. Never did he force his faith on any player, but he wanted each player to see the importance and the prominence of Jesus Christ in his life. It was a very sad day when the administration at the academy told Fisher that he no longer could lead our team in prayer before or after games. Not being able to share his prayers with his players hurt Fisher more than any loss on the football field ever could.

After each game, Fisher still told the players the same things he always did: "Call your parents if they're not here and tell them you love them and are thankful for their terrific support of you. If you go out, remember who you are. Don't do anything that would embarrass our team or school or distract us from our focus. And remember that tomorrow is the Lord's Day. Go to the church of your choice and thank God for the opportunity to attend the Air Force Academy and play this great game of college football."

Fisher undoubtedly will be remembered as the greatest coach in the history of service-academy football, but the people who really know Fisher will tell you that he is one of the greatest human beings in the history of college athletics. When I think of Fisher, I think of the countless times he would pull out a card during a staff meeting and tell us about someone who was ill or had lost a loved one and say how he thought it would be a nice thing to write that person a note of encouragement.

Fisher DeBerry impacted more lives through his coaching, through his power of influence, than he will ever know. His influence will continue to have a great impact on his players and their families for the rest of their lives. His influence will be seen throughout the coaching profession for many years to come. His influence definitely made a tremendous impact on my life and on my new role as the director of high school relations for the University of Arkansas football program. I thank God that I was given the opportunity to be a part of Fisher's team at the Air Force Academy.

Chapter Thirty-Two

STEVE RUSS

Linebacker
Three-year letterman (1992–94)
Graduated in 1995
Hometown: Stetsonville, Wis.
Resides now: Winston-Salem, N.C.

WHEN HE WAS AN AIR FORCE FRESHMAN, STEVE TOLD ME THE MOST IMPORTANT THINGS IN HIS LIFE WERE HIS RELATIONSHIP WITH GOD, THE LOVE HE HAD FOR HIS FAMILY AND HIS LOVE OF LIFTING WEIGHTS. HE DIDN'T GO TO HIS HIGH SCHOOL PROM HIS SENIOR YEAR BECAUSE HE WANTED TO LIFT WEIGHTS INSTEAD. I KNEW RIGHT THERE THAT STEVE WAS MY KIND OF FOOTBALL PLAYER. STEVE HAD A GREAT CAREER AS A LINEBACKER FOR THE FALCONS AND WENT ON TO HAVE A FINE CAREER IN THE NFL, EARNING TWO SUPER BOWL CHAMPIONSHIP RINGS WITH THE DENVER BRONCOS. HE'S COACHING TODAY WITH JIM GROBE AND STEED LOBOTZKE AT WAKE FOREST. STEVE HAS SO MUCH TO OFFER KIDS. HE IS GOING TO BE A GREAT HEAD COACH SOMEDAY.

I played in the NFL for two Super Bowl championship teams as a Denver Bronco, but it's what Coach DeBerry and Air Force football taught me that had the biggest impact on my life during my second career as a college football coach. I believe Fisher DeBerry's passion, attention to detail and organization, and the great assistant coaches he chose to surround himself with were his greatest strengths. These characteristics made Coach DeBerry stand among his peers across the country.

Anyone who has spent time with Coach DeBerry knows that his legendary fire burns bright. He coached with infectious enthusiasm and was always upbeat. Each time he talked to the team, no matter how he chose to deliver his message, there never was a doubt that he was speaking from a heart of great passion and conviction about the game he loved. He also introduced his players to his other passions. His faith is very important to him, and when I was a young cadet, that became evident by the way he conducted himself on and off the field, as well as how he lived his life. It inspired many of us to find out more and live a better life.

Coach DeBerry believed wholeheartedly in the importance of family and would always ask me how my mother and father were doing. He talked to the team about his wonderful wife, Lu Ann, and we could all see they had a terrific relationship — and still do. He also truly believed in the vital mission of the Air Force Academy. The all-important ideals of service before self, commitment to excellence, sacrifice and honor weren't just buzzwords to him when he was coaching. He wanted good football players, sure. But more than that, he wanted us to be great people. In his mind, as well as my own, there is no better leadership laboratory than the game of football — and the Air Force Academy is all about leadership.

Coach DeBerry loved lists. Players joked about how he would check each item off his list when he spoke to the team, usually with two very emphatic check marks! He always knew what the team needed to hear, and often they were the little things that would help us beat a superior opponent. His pregame talks to us at the team hotel covered each facet of the next day's game; no detail was too small.

You never had to wonder what Coach DeBerry really believed in. He would talk to us about the same things over and over and over. At the time, I thought Coach DeBerry was just getting more mileage out of an old speech. Now that I'm involved in coaching, I see that if you aren't talking about things on a daily basis that are important to you, well, they probably aren't all that important to you. Now, I couldn't agree more with Coach DeBerry, and my players are subjected to many of the same ideals. Through his preparation, organization and attention to

detail, Coach DeBerry produced some of the best college football teams in the
nation on a consistent basis.

In classic style, Coach DeBerry reminds us, "You are who you associate with,
men." Coach DeBerry surrounded himself with some of the finest, most loyal,
hardworking, caring and dedicated assistant coaches in the business. In the world
of college football coaching, many teams experience rapid rates of staff turnover
because assistants frequently move from job to job with little time for them to
unpack, let alone grow roots. But with Coach DeBerry, he treated his assistants so
well, staff openings were rare. He surrounded himself with men who shared many
of his beliefs about the right way to live and the right way to coach. It was easy for
Coach DeBerry's assistants to buy into and spread his message because they truly
believed in what he, and they, stood for. I'm working for one of those great men
right now, Jim Grobe at Wake Forest.

When you look at Coach DeBerry's coaching tree and how long his staff
members stayed with him, it's very revealing. Just on the defensive staff alone
when I played for the Falcons, Cal McCombs, Jim Grobe, Bill Stewart and Tom
Miller were all with Coach DeBerry for more than 10 years. When three of them
eventually left, they did so to become head coaches. The staff on the offensive
side of the ball was similar. This kind of loyalty from so many great coaches simply
can't be bought; it has to be earned. I've always believed that was the biggest
indicator of the type of person Coach DeBerry is.

Fisher DeBerry was extremely influential in my desire to become a college
football coach and was one of the first people I talked to when I was considering
coaching as a career. Coach DeBerry gave me great advice and told me that you
will receive much more from the game of football than you could ever hope to
give. He said the bonds you develop — and the positive impact you make on the
players — will become as precious to you as any number of wins you can attain.
Believe me, Coach DeBerry was right on the mark, and I have to thank him for
encouraging me to move my life in this direction. Whenever I'm with my players,
from time to time I will pause and smile because what just came out of my mouth
sounded exactly like Coach DeBerry — minus the Southern drawl, of course. It's
a wonderful reminder of a great man who has had so much to do with my life, at
the Air Force Academy and beyond.

Chapter Thirty-Three

KEN RUCKER

Running backs coach (1984–89)
Hometown: Morristown, Tenn.
Resides now: Austin, Texas

KEN IS A MAN I GREATLY RESPECT AND ADMIRE. WE WERE ON THE STAFF TOGETHER AS ASSISTANT COACHES AT APPALACHIAN STATE. I KNEW KEN HAD HIS PRIORITIES IN THE RIGHT ORDER AND THAT HE WOULD BE ONE OF THE FIRST PEOPLE I WOULD CONTACT IF I EVER GOT A HEAD COACHING JOB. THAT'S WHAT I DID, AND THE JOB HE DID FOR HIS PLAYERS AT AIR FORCE MADE HIM ONE OF THE MOST RESPECTED AND SOUGHT-AFTER ASSISTANT COACHES IN THE NATION. HIS PRIORITIES OF FAITH, FAMILY AND FOOTBALL HAVE HAD A GREAT INFLUENCE ON ME. EVERYONE LOVES COACH RUCKER, A TRUE PLAYER'S COACH. WHAT A DIFFERENCE HE'S MAKING TODAY IN THE LIVES OF SO MANY OUTSTANDING PLAYERS AT TEXAS.

Coach DeBerry's remarkable success at Air Force, built during his 23 years as head coach, didn't happen by accident. There is a legacy everyone needs to know.

Fisher and I, and our families, go way back to our Appalachian State

181

days. In 1979, Fisher's college coach at Wofford and head football coach at Appalachian State in Boone, N.C., was the late Jim Brakefield. Coach Brakefield hired me for my first job in collegiate coaching. As assistant coaches at Appalachian State, Fisher and I would begin a lifelong friendship. Fisher began showing me how to be personable in recruiting and how to be a strong, positive influence in the lives of the players I coached. Fisher would collect newspapers during the week, and while traveling to play that weekend, he would cut out articles and handwrite letters to each recruit. That personal approach to recruiting inspires me to this day.

One of the best telephone calls I ever received came in December 1983. By then, Fisher was offensive coordinator at Air Force, and I was coaching at Richmond for Dal Shealy, my former college coach. My phone rang, and it was Fisher on the line. Fisher had worked with me only one year at Appalachian State before moving to Colorado Springs in 1980 to be a part of Kenny Hatfield's coaching staff. When he called me, Fisher had just been promoted to head coach as the replacement for Coach Hatfield, who left for Arkansas after leading Air Force to a 10-2 record in 1983. Fisher offered me a job on his staff, and I jumped at the chance. He wanted me to help him and his staff continue to build what you see today, one of the best college football programs in America, which is now in the capable hands of Fisher's successor, Troy Calhoun.

Fisher built a terrific program at the Air Force Academy and did it the right way, with good people and strong values. He put together a great staff — guys who will remain friends for life. They include the late Bruce Johnson, a great defensive coordinator we miss dearly; and Jim Grobe, who made Wake Forest football a power program as Wake's head coach. Others were Dick Enga, Tom Miller, Billy Mitchell, Dick Ellis, Charlie Weatherbie (the former Navy head coach now doing another fine job at Louisiana-Monroe), Sammy Steinmark, Cal McCombs, Carl Rusk, Darrell Mastin and Mike Gould. You don't just forget wonderful people like that. Influential men filled the ranks of support roles as well; among them were Jack Braley, Jim Conboy and Jack Culliton.

I chose coaching as my profession to influence kids. I aim to make an impact, not just an impression. My mother was a huge influence in my life, along with my high school coach, the late Rex Dockery. I had a cousin, the late Charles Rucker, who introduced me to football when I was in the fourth grade. He was my first coach, my first mentor on the field. These men individually guided me into coaching and led me to coach at the Air Force Academy, a special place my family and I will never forget.

To this day, representing the Air Force Academy has helped me so much in recruiting when I enter schools and homes and people's lives. Coaching at Air Force helped me build self-esteem, integrity and character. You truly are representing excellence in life when you are recruiting for the Falcons.

After stops at Baylor, North Carolina, Arkansas, Texas A&M and Georgia to spread my coaching wings, I now work for the University of Texas and head coach Mack Brown. After coaching the Texas running backs for three seasons, which included the thrill of being part of the 2005 national championship team, I moved into an exciting new position with the Longhorns as director of high school relations and player development. Coach Brown and Texas stand for the same excellence as Air Force, so it's been a great fit for me in Austin.

My faith has encouraged me each time adversity has struck. I recently overcame prostate cancer and have a strong belief that God's plan has me here today. That encouragement took root during my time at Air Force, working with Fisher and our great staff and being around all those wonderful cadets we were fortunate to have as players. I can't think of a single Air Force player I coached who hasn't been a positive influence in my life. That's how great those kids were. I'm blessed to remain in touch with many of them. I'm so proud of them all and the outstanding men they became. May God continue to bless them.

At game-day breakfasts, Coach DeBerry would open by saying, "This is the day the Lord has made. Let us rejoice and be glad in it." I still use and am guided by those words today, as I rejoice in God and His love for all of us.

Chapter Thirty-Four

Capt. Chance Harridge

Quarterback
Three-year letterman (2001–03)
Graduated in 2004
Hometown: Bonaire, Ga.
Resides now: Charleston, S.C.

POUND FOR POUND, CHANCE WAS PROBABLY THE MOST COMPETITIVE PLAYER I EVER COACHED. HE WASN'T AFRAID OF ANYBODY OR ANYTHING. THAT'S WHAT YOU NEED FROM YOUR QUARTERBACK. CHANCE'S TEAMMATES HAD SUCH GREAT RESPECT AND HIGH REGARD FOR HIM. I WILL NEVER FORGET HIS REMARKS TO THE TEAM AFTER WE BEAT CALIFORNIA 23-21 IN BERKELEY IN 2002. CHANCE TOLD THE TEAM, "THERE IS SOMETHING SPECIAL IN THIS ROOM. THAT'S WHY WE WON." HIS COMMENTS PERSONIFIED THE BROTHERHOOD CONCEPT THAT IS THE FOUNDATION OF AIR FORCE FOOTBALL.

After all these years, I still don't have the words to properly express my gratitude for the experiences and the life the good Lord has blessed me with as a result of attending the Air Force Academy and playing football for Coach DeBerry and the Air Force Falcons.

Now that I'm a student pilot at Vance Air Force Base in Oklahoma, where I am the senior ranking officer of my class and am flying the T-1 Jayhawk trainer, I can't begin to tell you how much pilot training resembles life at the academy on and off the field. I've had a taste of both Navy and Air Force training; both expect and demand your very best. In training, there are daily rides that lead up to check rides to ensure proficiency in each stage of flying. It's very much like football, where everything you do in practice leads up to game day, and the results are in direct proportion to what you invested.

Coach DeBerry always stressed to his players that "we are going to be an effort" football team. That statement runs parallel to what I am doing today. I wasn't the biggest, most athletic guy ever to wear the Air Force lightning bolt, and I'm not the smartest guy in pilot training. But there are a few constants I do have control over: my attitude and my effort. My goals as a player and now as a student pilot are the same: I want everyone around me to say that I'm always prepared and have a great attitude. If you have those things going for you, the results will take care of themselves.

Anyone who knows me knows that I'm hardheaded, so I've learned a lot about who I am and who I want to become through growing experiences. With every passing day, I have the responsibility to make the choice to do what's right. Coach DeBerry had one rule for his players: Do what's right! Today is no different. I wake up every morning and make a decision to be a better person than I was yesterday. If I fail, I know who I'm responsible to, and I take it up with him. Coach DeBerry always cared more about the men we were going to become than the boys we were playing football. For that reason, I have the utmost respect for the man. I hope as I grow older that my priorities will be the same.

Through football, I learned how to deal with unexpected, abrupt changes to my optimal plans. For me, there's nothing more unsettling than mission planning for a few hours and then being told in a briefing, "We aren't going to do that today. How about this?" You try to make everything as perfect as possible — and on paper, it is — only to be told it's not good enough because of airport runway closures, weather, or other factors.

The same holds true in football. There's nothing more unsettling than game planning and watching film of your opponent all week for, say, a 4-3 defense, cover 2, and then showing up Saturday, game day, and the opponent is running some version of an eight-man defensive front with cover 3 in the secondary. This is why we practice — in flying and in football — because the weather forecaster doesn't always give us clear conditions, nor does the opposing defensive coordinator give us what we expect. One of my mom's favorite Coach DeBerry quotes is "We can't control what happens to us today, but we can control how we react to those things." He told us that a million times. And every time he said it, it was just as true and just as important to remember as the first time he said it.

My flying experiences are limited because I'm a student pilot, but where football is concerned, there is always a big dose of adversity come game day. A perfect example came in the 2002 season, my junior year. We had gotten off to a hot start, beating Northwestern (52-3) and New Mexico (38-31 in overtime) at Falcon Stadium and upsetting 23rd-ranked California (23-21) at Berkeley. California, led by Kyle Boller, had blown out Baylor (70-22) to open the season and was coming off a big victory at Michigan State (46-22) when we beat the Bears in Berkeley. On film, the Bears were big and fast. Game day proved that was no myth. So we were 3-0 and rolling when we arrived in Salt Lake City to play Utah.

We jumped out to a 6-0 lead over the Utes, only to find ourselves trailing 26-6 at halftime. Suddenly we were playing awful football. I will never forget Coach DeBerry's halftime speech to us. "Men, if you don't believe you are going to win this game, I can walk across the way and let them know we will forfeit the second half," he said. "We have everything we need in this room to win the game. Don't walk out of this locker room if you think it's over." It was probably one of his shortest halftime speeches, but there wasn't much to say. We were embarrassed because we hadn't played well, and we didn't think the Utes were that great a team. We practically gave them two touchdowns with our turnovers and penalties.

But the second half of the game seemed to come straight out of Hollywood. We chopped wood and finally got our offense moving, and our defense played lights out. We were still down 26-23 when we got the ball back with less than two minutes left. We weren't playing to kick a tying field goal, either. We were going for the win. I wasn't much of a passer, but one of my better-thrown balls was a 20-yard strike that went to Don Clark for the winning touchdown with 17 seconds left. We went from trailing 26-6 at halftime to winning 30-26. Up in our radio booth, play-by-play man Jim Arthur was screaming, "Air Force wins! Air Force wins! Air Force wins!" Our postgame celebration was spectacular, and so was the silence from a shocked Utah crowd.

My high school coach was the first person who asked me if I would be interested in playing for a service academy. My reaction: "Service academy?" When I learned that Air Force plays Division I-A football, I became interested. Playing major college football was all I wanted to do since I started playing at 6 years of age.

Pretty soon, Coach DeBerry came recruiting. He wanted to know my thoughts about coming to Colorado Springs and being an option quarterback for the Falcons. He asked if I had ever been out west. I replied, "Yes, sir, I have been. My baseball team played in a tournament in Birmingham, Alabama." Coach DeBerry still laughs when he tells that story.

After my official recruiting visit to the academy, it was time to make the most important decision of my life — go or no go — and I was scared to death. I was going to have to attend the Air Force Prep School first, and that didn't sit well with me. My mom and dad thought it was the greatest idea ever. But I was 18, and I did the simple math: Five years at the academy plus five years of military service equals 10 years, which would take me to age 28. Yikes! Thankfully, I made the right choice. I did the right thing. And to this day, it's absolutely the best decision I've ever made.

Chuck Petersen, my offensive coordinator and my quarterbacks coach at Air Force, was my best friend on the field. There was no fooling Coach Pete. We were honest with each other, we were blunt and we both demanded the best of each other. During spring ball of my freshman year, I jumped from No. 5 on the depth chart all the way up to No. 1. When you're the No. 5 quarterback, you sit through meetings and try to understand what's going on in all the schemes. When you're the No. 1 quarterback, everyone looks to you because you should know it all.

I survived spring camp and was heading into my sophomore season as the No. 1 guy. What I failed to realize was that as the starting quarterback, I was expected to help my teammates win. The majority of a young quarterback's time should be spent at the chalkboard and in the film room, because nothing is more embarrassing than showing up in the fall and getting yelled at on the field for not "pitching off support." It was a humbling experience to go from starter to backup so quickly after rising so fast to be the No. 1 guy, but my sophomore year was the year I really grew up as a football player.

My parents still have the biggest influence on my life. I've always appreciated how hard they worked to provide everything my brother and I needed to succeed. My parents taught me that family and love are the most important things in life.

They also taught me that if you're going to do something, do it with all your heart, with all that you are, to make it the best. I enjoy an amazing relationship with my parents and can't say "Thank you" and "I love you" enough to them.

Never allow challenges — in sports, work, family or life — to beat you down and leave you there. Your mind and spirit can rise above and overcome anything.

Chapter Thirty-Five

CHAD HENNINGS

———

Defensive tackle
Four-year letterman (1984–87)
Graduated in 1988
Hometown: Elberon, Iowa
Resides now: Flower Mound, Texas

———

CHAD WAS UNQUESTIONABLY THE MOST COMPLETE AND THE MOST OUTSTANDING PLAYER WE HAD DURING MY CAREER AT THE ACADEMY. GOD BLESSED HIM WITH OUTSTANDING ABILITY, AND ONCE HE REALIZED THAT, HIS CAREER REALLY TOOK OFF. BUT CHAD WAS ALSO ONE OF THE HARDEST WORKERS WHO HAS EVER BEEN A PART OF AIR FORCE FOOTBALL. HE STARTED HIS CAREER AS A 213-POUND FRESHMAN TIGHT END. HE ENDED IT AS A 275-POUND CONSENSUS ALL-AMERICA DEFENSIVE TACKLE AND WINNER OF THE 1987 OUTLAND TROPHY, WHICH GOES TO THE NATION'S BEST LINEMAN. CHAD WAS ALSO AN ACADEMIC ALL-AMERICAN. CHAD WOULD BE THE FIRST TO GIVE CREDIT TO HIS FAMILY FOR THE WORK ETHIC HE LEARNED AT HOME ON THE FARM, TO HIS TEAMMATES AND COACHES, AND TO HIS MASTER COACH, JESUS CHRIST.

He fulfilled his dream of serving our country and flying combat missions before playing nine years in the NFL with the Dallas Cowboys and winning three Super Bowl championship rings. Now he has his own beautiful, loving family. He sets a great example for all of us by living the core values of the Air Force Academy on a daily basis.

———————

I was blessed to play nine years in the NFL, blessed to be a part of three Super Bowl championship teams with the Dallas Cowboys, blessed to be inducted into the College Football Hall of Fame. And yet the ring I cherish the most, the ring that represents my greatest achievement, is my Air Force Academy class ring.

Don't misunderstand me; all those other rings are very special to me. But my Air Force Academy class ring stands above the rest because of what it represents. The academy is where I became a man. It's where I grew the most spiritually, physically, emotionally and academically. Growing and maturing at the Air Force Academy set the stage for everything I've been able to do with my life. That's my ringing endorsement of the academy and of playing football for the Falcons.

Because of my high school wrestling commitments, I was the last football recruit of my class to be brought in. I'm lucky Coach DeBerry and the Falcons waited for me, because I couldn't imagine missing out on such a great opportunity. I'm a big believer in Providence, and I'm convinced I was meant to attend the Air Force Academy. Yet like all fourth-class cadets, my first year at the academy was extremely difficult. You naturally think about leaving, about going to another school where life is so much easier.

During spring break of my freshman year, I went to visit some friends at Arizona State. I remember saying to myself, "This would be a great place to go to school." And then I never gave it another thought, because I just couldn't quit what I had started. That was a big rule in our family when I was growing up in rural Iowa on a 900-acre farm. My parents, Bill and Barb Hennings, wouldn't allow any of us to quit anything we started. "Once you start something, you finish it," my parents always told us. So that's what I did. Even after my sophomore year, when you can leave the academy with no penalty of financial compensation to the government for the cost of your first two years of education, I never considered leaving. I was fully committed to finishing what I started, and I'm still benefiting from that today.

I was a blue-collar player. Yes, I was blessed with talent. We're all blessed with talent. But talent alone doesn't get you very far without a strong work ethic. Your work ethic is your separation factor. If you work hard, you will be more successful in life than people who don't work hard. My family's farm near tiny Elberon (pop. 150) was the perfect training camp for building a strong work ethic. After baling hay and working the fields for six or seven hours with my older brother, Todd, he took me to our high school athletic facilities for a workout. This was our routine every day. Todd helped me realize the importance of never skipping a workout. He also helped me understand that you can always fit more work into your day's schedule, even when you're dead tired after doing farm chores.

My father was fond of saying, "We don't eat if we don't do the work." That's so true of life on a farm. When you think about it, this applies in every walk of life. There's no sense of accomplishment without the hard work that comes with it. If you want to be a success in life, you had better be willing to do the work to make that happen.

Don't wait for somebody else, for the other team, to make your breaks for you. My sophomore year at Air Force, the 1985 season, we were playing Notre Dame at Falcon Stadium and trailing late in a nationally televised game with a record home crowd watching. That was the season we started 10-0, but we were really up against it on that October day. Notre Dame was moving the ball, looking for more points to put us away. But we refused to lose. Terry Maki, our terrific linebacker, blocked a field goal, and A.J. Scott returned the ball for the winning touchdown. We found a way to win. To me, that game best displayed one of the most important core components of Coach DeBerry's football program: You never quit. You never die.

Any football award, any military honor I've received wouldn't have been possible without the help of my great Air Force teammates, my great Air Force coaches and all the great airmen in my squadrons. When I enrolled at the academy, my only goal was to be the very best cadet and the very best football player I could be, and then the very best officer I could be. You just don't come to the Air Force Academy planning to win the Outland Trophy, planning to be inducted into the College Football Hall of Fame, planning to play in the NFL. I had no idea any of that was in my future. But I was fortunate to find myself surrounded in the classroom and on the football field by the best people you could ever want to meet. I couldn't have done any of it without their help and guidance.

It makes me feel good when somebody says, "Hey, you're Chad Hennings. You played for the Dallas Cowboys." But it makes me feel *great* when somebody says, "Hey, you're Chad Hennings. You played at the Air Force Academy and flew combat missions before you played for the Dallas Cowboys." I'm proud of my Air Force career, at the academy and beyond. Before I played in the NFL, I flew 45 missions in an A-10 Thunderbolt over northern Iraq, helping to provide relief and humanitarian aid to Kurdish refugees. I'm proud that I chose a path of service before I chose a football career. I want my life to be about service before self.

In the universal battle of riches versus wealth, I strive for wealth, which means having strong character, principles and eternal values. I want my children — my son Chase is 16 and my daughter Brenna is 12 — to think of their father as much more than just a football player. They will become better people knowing that my wife, Tammy, and I are big believers in serving others before serving yourself. You should always be in a personal-growth mode. You try to learn from the people you emulate, and you should pass on those important life lessons to everyone around you.

My extended family members are my Air Force teammates. I wouldn't hesitate to call any of them in a time of need, knowing they would move mountains to offer help. That's the result of the unique bond Air Force players develop. When I think of Coach DeBerry's staff, I think of great Christian people completely dedicated to their coaching profession and to mentoring and molding young men into leaders.

Troy Calhoun, who was one of my Air Force teammates, is the perfect fit as Coach DeBerry's successor. Air Force football continues to be in great hands with Troy now in charge of the program as the Falcons' head coach. Coaching at the academy can't be easy, because the players are pulled in so many directions with all their academic and military commitments. But I can't imagine another place where coaching is more rewarding. As an Air Force Academy graduate, Troy gets it. He understands the mission of the academy. He wants to win as much as any coach and will work as hard as he can to make that happen, but I think his true passion is molding young men into leaders for our country.

I was one of those young men many years ago, and I am the forever-thankful beneficiary of that marvelous molding.

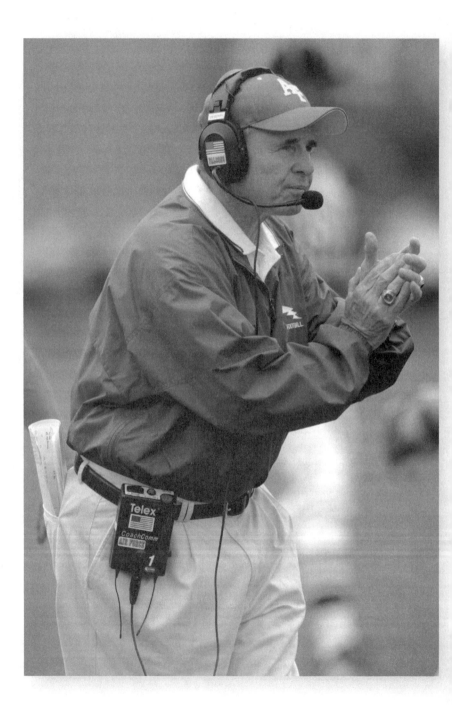

Conclusion

Fisher DeBerry

─────

There comes a time in our lives when we all must answer a very important question: What do I want my legacy to be?

I don't think life is about how many games you win, how much money you make or how many important positions you hold. My philosophy of coaching was influenced by three great men: Jim Brakefield, Jim Bowman and Kenny Hatfield. Hanging on a wall in my Air Force Academy office was a statement of my philosophy and reason for coaching: "Success in coaching is not measured by the number of wins and losses. Real success in coaching is measured by the men your players become." It gives me enormous pride to see the many wonderful things former Air Force players and coaches are doing with their lives and how they are influencing others by serving our nation in the military, by working in the corporate world, by coaching and by being loving husbands and fathers.

I chose to coach because I wanted to help young people get an education. After all, there were so many people who helped me in my pursuit of education, so many people who created terrific opportunities for me. I call it a give-back attitude. My greatest satisfaction in life is seeing young people perform and have success in the endeavors they choose. Seeing kids happy and proud of themselves and seeing them reach goals they once thought would be impossible to reach — that is my real joy.

The ability to love and care about people other than yourself is the key to being a successful coach or mentor. If your players know that you genuinely care about them and have their welfare at the top of your list of priorities, they will give you all they have in effort. Every play, every game, every day. I hope my players felt that way about me, and I hope this is part of the legacy I left for them: to influence others.

We all have the power to make a difference in the lives of others. We just need to listen to our Master Coach, who encourages us to "let your light shine." That light is the power of influence. Young people today, more than ever, need positive role models to guide them through life.

I recently spoke in Alabama at a Fellowship of Christian Athletes luncheon for high school coaches. At the conclusion of my talk, a coach told me that he had been a player on a team that the Falcons had played in the Liberty Bowl. That particular year, he listened to Lance McDowell, one of our quarterbacks, speak at the Liberty Bowl's FCA breakfast. This coach shared with me how the words (the seeds) of Lance had impacted his life. That breakfast took place nearly 20 years ago, yet the high school coach still remembered Lance's words.

The coach shared with me how he had lived his dream, first as a great high school player, and then as an all-conference player in college. He even ended up with an opportunity to play in the NFL. But he still felt emptiness in his heart. He said Lance's testimony inspired him to go to seminary and then to preaching God's love in a church. Still, he felt God prompting him elsewhere. He made the decision to go into education and become a football coach at a Christian school. The significance he yearned for in his life was inspired by Lance at that FCA breakfast so long ago. Now he is seeing dramatic changes in the lives of young people that God has entrusted to him. It's another classic example that we never know the seeds we sow.

One of the best tributes I've ever heard paid to a man's life was expressed by Brian Cabral, the longtime linebackers coach at the University of Colorado. Brian's tribute was to his former college coach, Dan Stavely. I referred to Dan as "Mr. FCA in Colorado." Dan probably influenced the lives of more young people in Colorado than any person I have ever known.

On the night of Dan's retirement, Brian stood and paid tribute to him by saying, "Coach, I've never met, nor have I ever seen, nor have I ever heard a man more Christ-like than you." This is the type of influence we should all try to be to others. Dan obviously had sown wonderful seeds in Brian's heart. This should be the challenge for all of us, to be more Christ-like in our relationships. This is the ultimate example of the real power of influence.

My good friend Rudy Ruettiger, of Notre Dame fame and the hit movie "Rudy," likes to say, "We only have one life to live. Make it count."

What do you want your legacy to be?

GRANT TEAFF

Executive director
American Football Coaches Association
Waco, Texas

W E ALL HAVE HEROES, AND GRANT IS ONE OF MY COACHING HEROES.
SOON AFTER I BECAME AIR FORCE'S HEAD COACH, I WENT TO
BAYLOR TO VISIT WITH GRANT AND HIS COACHING STAFF. MUCH OF
GRANT'S PROGRAM AT BAYLOR WAS REFLECTED IN OUR PROGRAM AT AIR
FORCE BECAUSE OF THE RESPECT I GAINED FOR GRANT AS A HUSBAND, A
FATHER AND A COACH. HE IS TRULY WHAT IT MEANS TO BE A CHRISTIAN
COACH, A MAN WHO PUTS HIS PLAYERS AND OTHERS BEFORE HIMSELF.
HE WAS A GREAT COACH ON THE FIELD, AS ANY BAYLOR FAN CAN TELL
YOU, BUT HIS EFFORT IN BUILDING THE AMERICAN FOOTBALL COACHES
ASSOCIATION INTO ONE OF THE FINEST ORGANIZATIONS IN THIS COUNTRY IS
HIS CROWNING JEWEL.

My 6-year-old grandson, Eli Pittman, came running into our home wearing
his Tim Duncan jersey. (Duncan is No. 21 with the San Antonio Spurs of

the NBA). Eli is a ball of energy, with a head covered in ultra-blond, earlobe-length hair. His hair has been that way for most of his 6 years, which caused his proclamation to me to be even more amazing. He proudly announced that he was going to get a Tim Duncan haircut to go with his Tim Duncan jersey.

Here is a young boy who has seen Tim Duncan play with the Spurs one time, watched him on television and in turn adopted him as someone to emulate. The two most obvious and recognizable aspects of Tim Duncan are his No. 21 jersey and his quarter-inch-long hair. As a grandfather, I hope Eli will copy many more of Tim's values and his work ethic.

I once heard a prominent NBA player state clearly, "I am not a role model for the youth of America." My experience tells me that particular NBA player was totally wrong. Whether he wants to be or not, he is a role model and an influence, as we all are. The question always is, Will that influence be positive or negative?

I was greatly influenced by my family as I watched them live out the values they taught. My high school coaches and teachers not only taught me how to win; they influenced me to become a coach and teacher. I coached for 37 years — including 21 years as the head football coach at Baylor University, from 1972-92 — and not a day goes by that I don't hear from someone whom I had the privilege of coaching or teaching. They write, they call and they send e-mail to relay to me the impact they believe I had on their lives. What a great feeling to realize that many of those you deliberately tried to impact and influence actually got it.

For the last 15 years, I have been the executive director of the American Football Coaches Association. When I took that position of leadership, my goals were relatively simple. I wanted to build an organization that could promote and protect our great game. We would also provide educational and development opportunities for those who coach the game. We strive daily through the educational venues, publications, Web site and national convention to emphasize to coachs that through their influence, they can have a positive impact on a young person's life above and beyond the football field.

To remind AFCA members about their responsibility to mentor and lead in a positive way, the American Football Coaches Foundation selects a single high school coach to receive America's most prestigious award: the Power of Influence Award. Each high school coaches association in all 50 states can select one outstanding high school coach from their state to be considered for the honor. The nominees are pared down to a final five for the foundation's board of directors to evaluate and choose a winner. The criteria for selection are largely based on the influence that the coach has on his team, on his community and within our profession. We have discovered that those who exhibit the most positive influence also have the most impressive wins.

In 2001, after putting the finishing touches on the beautiful new AFCA national headquarters in Waco, Texas, my wife, Donell and I traveled to New York City for the College Football Foundation Hall of Fame ceremonies. During that special and memorable time, I reflected on how I got to be selected for the College Football Hall of Fame. My answer was clear: It was the power of influence. My high school coaches taught me how to play the game and live life the right way, and my college coaches greatly influenced me in how to coach the game the right way. Many assistant coaches throughout my career also influenced me with their great intensity and compassion. The power of influence began to manifest in my mind through the faces of hundreds of coaches whom I had come in contact with throughout the years. Then one clear thought emerged: All of us in the coaching profession were first taught to play the game, and then we had the great honor and privilege of teaching the game to those in our charge.

The morning after the hall of fame induction, Donell and I went for a walk and passed by a store that sold fine artwork. There in the window looking out at me was a statue of a young boy. He held a football tightly in his small hand and a football helmet in the other. I looked into the boy's eyes, and he seemed to say to me what I said to my own high school coach: "Teach me to play the game and teach me how to live life." I walked into the store, bought the statue and had it shipped to Waco because it symbolized all that I believed about the power of influence. On the plane ride back to Texas, I sat quietly writing a poem in my attempt to explain this.

A Coach's Influence

I dreamed a dream, but I had my doubts.
"You can do it," he said. "I'll teach you how."
I tried and tried, he said I should.
I gave it my best, he knew I would.
Lessons taught on the field of strife,
Have been invaluable, as I have faced life.
When challenges come my way,
I always think, what would he say?

His inspiring words I hear even now,
"You can do it. I taught you how."
Now, others dream, and have their doubts.
I say, "You can do it. I'll teach you how."
The influence continues.

On that plane ride back home, an idea to honor coaches was born, which came to fruition through the building of the American Football Coaches Plaza of Influence at our facility. This plaza is a special place where football coaches can be honored by those whose lives they have inspired. Coaches range from the obscure to the nationally known. The common bond is their profound influence on lives touched and changed.

When I decided to give up football coaching at the end of the 1992 season, I had been serving as the athletic director and the head football coach at Baylor. I felt that for the future of Baylor athletics, I needed to commit my time to being the athletic director. At the end of the 1992 season, I coached my last game in the Sun Bowl against Arizona. We won 20-15 to complete a 7-5 season.

At that time, the leadership of the American Football Coaches Association approached me about becoming the executive director upon the retirement of Charlie McClendon. I had been heavily involved with the AFCA through the years and was serving as a member of the board of trustees as well as the chairman of the ethics committee. Of course I had a great love and passion for our great game and for coaching. Fisher DeBerry, who was on the board and was a coach for whom I had great respect and admiration, asked me to come to the Air Force Academy to speak to his team and staff. He was on the AFCA's executive committee, which led the search for the new executive director.

Coach DeBerry and I spent several hours during my time at the Air Force Academy talking about the AFCA. I was impressed with the board's compelling arguments and rationale for offering me the position. Coach DeBerry influenced my decision strongly with his commitment to do everything in his power to help me implement the plans I deemed necessary to take the AFCA where it needed to go. He backed up those words of support through his presidency of the AFCA board and later accepting responsibility as chairman of the ethics committee.

Coach DeBerry is typical of those who commit their lives to the coaching profession. Long ago, his football coaches taught him to play the game of football and to live life the right way. He, in turn, passed this legacy on to countless others. This book is not the summation of the power of Fisher DeBerry's influence, because it would take volumes to do so. Rather, it contains a few testimonials from a small number of us whose lives he has touched through his power of influence.

I would be remiss if I did not say that as coaches, the vast majority of us are blessed to have a powerful influence in our own lives — an influence constantly with us, win or lose, during long nights after a loss and in moments of sheer joy. For Fisher, that person is his wife, Lu Ann. It's often said that when coaches marry, they outkick their coverage. Fisher certainly did.

Fisher DeBerry's influence continues.

Fisher DeBerry

Year by Year as Air Force Head Football Coach

YEAR	OVERALL	VS. NAVY	VS. ARMY	CONFERENCE	FINISH	BOWL GAME
1984	8-4	W, 29-22	L, 24-12	4-3	3rd	Independence vs. Virginia Tech (W, 23-7)
x-1985	12-1	W, 24-7	W, 45-7	7-1	t-1st	Bluebonnet vs. Texas (W, 24-16)
1986	6-5	W, 40-6	L, 21-11	5-2	3rd	
1987	9-4	W, 23-13	W, 27-10	6-2	3rd	Freedom vs. Arizona State (L, 33-28)
1988	5-7	W, 34-24	L, 28-15	3-5	t-6th	
1989	8-4-1	W, 35-7	W, 29-3	5-1-1	2nd	Liberty vs. Mississippi (L, 42-29)
1990	7-5	W, 24-7	W, 15-3	3-4	6th	Liberty vs. Ohio State (W, 23-11)
1991	10-3	W, 46-6	W, 25-0	6-2	3rd	Liberty vs. Mississippi State (W, 38-15)
1992	7-5	W, 18-16	W, 7-3	4-4	t-5th	Liberty vs. Mississippi (L, 13-0)
1993	4-8	L, 28-24	W, 25-6	1-7	9th	
1994	8-4	W, 43-21	W, 10-6	6-2	t-2nd	
x-1995	8-5	W, 30-20	W, 38-20	6-2	t-1st	Copper vs. Texas Tech (L, 55-41)
1996	6-5	L, 20-17	L, 23-7	5-3	4th	
1997	10-3	W, 10-7	W, 24-0	6-2	2nd	Las Vegas vs. Oregon (L, 41-13)
y-1998	12-1	W, 49-7	W, 35-7	7-1	1st	Oahu vs. Washington (W, 45-25)
1999	6-5	W, 19-14	W, 28-0	2-5	7th	
2000	9-3	W, 27-13	W, 41-27	5-2	2nd	Silicon Valley vs. Fresno State (W, 37-34)
2001	6-6	W, 24-18	W, 34-24	3-4	t-5th	
2002	8-5	W, 48-7	W, 49-30	4-3	t-3rd	San Francisco vs. Virginia Tech (L, 20-13)
2003	7-5	L, 28-25	W, 31-3	3-4	t-4th	
2004	5-6	L, 24-21	W, 31-22	3-4	t-4th	
2005	4-7	L, 27-24	L, 27-24	3-5	7th	
2006	4-8	L, 24-17	W, 43-7	3-5	t-6th	
Total	169-109-1	17-6	18-5	100-73-1		Bowls: 6-6

Western Athletic Conference, 1984 – 98
Mountain West Conference, 1999 – 2006
x-WAC co-champions
y-WAC champions

ALL PROCEEDS FROM THIS BOOK
BENEFIT THE FISHER DEBERRY FOUNDATION

The Fisher DeBerry Foundation is a tax-exempt, nonprofit organization dedicated to the support and education of single parents and their children, as well as other charitable causes. Founded by legendary and all-time winningest United States Air Force Academy head football coach Fisher DeBerry and his wife, Lu Ann, the Fisher DeBerry Foundation provides support for parenting development, mentoring programs, after-school activities and funding for academic scholarships.

Fisher DeBerry Foundation
8235 Loganwood Court
Colorado Springs, CO 80919
Phone: (877) 352-6224

www.fisherdeberryfoundation.org